ABANDONED
CLEVELAND
RUINS OF THE RUST BELT

KYLE BROOKY

AMERICA
THROUGH TIME®
ADDING COLOR TO AMERICAN HISTORY

America Through Time is an imprint of Fonthill Media LLC
www.through-time.com
office@through-time.com

Published by Arcadia Publishing by arrangement with Fonthill Media LLC
For all general information, please contact Arcadia Publishing:
Telephone: 843-853-2070
Fax: 843-853-0044
E-mail: sales@arcadiapublishing.com
For customer service and orders:
Toll-Free 1-888-313-2665

www.arcadiapublishing.com

First published 2020

Copyright © Kyle Brooky 2020

ISBN 978-1-63499-207-7

Typeset in Trade Gothic 10pt on 15pt
Printed and bound in England

CONTENTS

ABOUT THE AUTHOR

KYLE BROOKY has always been interested in the strange and offbeat. From a young age, he always wondered what lied within that "spooky old house" in the woods near his grandparents' cottage. In 2016, along with a partner, he formed Ruin Road, a video blog dedicated to exploring abandoned and forgotten buildings. Utilizing his media production degree, he has been dedicated to preserving these beautiful places through film and photographs to tell the history of these places that are now forgotten by most. In his spare time, he enjoys writing screenplays and collecting movies.

INTRODUCTION

T he land that would become Cuyahoga County was first inhabited year-round by Native Americans around the 1500s, drawn to the water, bountiful forests, and rich land. More tribes would move to the area and, in 1796, a European survey party would arrive with their leader, Moses Cleaveland. The settlement had just seven citizens in the 1800 Census. A decade later, that number reached fifty-seven, and in another decade, it had jumped to over 600.

With the construction of the Ohio & Erie Canal in 1827, businesses began to look at the area as a major transportation hub and ideal location for their operations. By 1880, the now-city of Cleveland was the twelfth largest in the nation. This rust-belt city was an ideal place for entrepreneurs, blue-collar workers, and immigrants hoping to find the American Dream. In 1920, Cleveland was the fifth-largest city in America.

But the good times could not last forever, and the city has suffered along the way. One in three working men were unemployed during the Great Depression, one of the worst rates in the nation. While the population would continue to rise, peaking in 1950, this was the start of the city's downfall. Each decade would see the city move down the ranks of largest in the nation.

The Cuyahoga River caught on fire in 1969 from the buildup of pollutants such as oil, just three years after the city itself had been set alight with violence and rioting during the Hough race riots. Residents who had once come to Cleveland with dreams of a better future were now fleeing in terror, leaving a crumbling city behind. With over thirty million dollars of debt by 1978, Cleveland became the first city to default on its loans since the Great Depression.

The city would not come out of default until 1987, but the damage was already done. In 2004, it earned the title of "poorest major city in America," which it would

receive again two years later. Seventeen percent of its population left between 2000 and 2010. The poverty rate was a staggering 32.4 percent. Foreclosures, closing businesses, and crime led to more than 120,000 abandoned buildings dotting the city like scars to remind those who remained.

Cleveland is a city that the rest of America and other countries can learn from. It is resilient. Since 1949, it has been named an All-American City five times, but those scars remain. The city is desperately trying to demolish its blighted buildings to reduce crime and attract new business, but at what cost? As you will see in the following chapters, these are not just places left for dust to pile and paint to flake, but are places that were once full of life. Where history has occurred, now forgotten and condemned, many now lost to the wrecking ball.

–1–
BUSINESS
AND INDUSTRY

Industry has always been at the heart of Cleveland and has been a primary factor in the city's growth and decline. The construction of the Ohio & Erie Canal in 1832 cemented the city's place as a major hub for transportation, both via land and water. With the canal, materials could be quickly transported to and from the city to any number of other locations along the lakes.

This transportation hub began to draw the attention of many businesses, in particular the iron industry, and just five years later as many as four iron foundries had opened to produce iron-based products such as steam engines for trains. The iron industry grew, becoming the most valuable industrial product in the city with twenty percent of the entire city's manufacturing dedicated solely to the metal.

This export also linked to the city's other businesses—for example, a great deal of iron sewing machines were made in Cleveland, which in turn saw many clothing companies based in the city, leading to the clothing industry becoming one of Cleveland's other major businesses.

The following years saw a number of other industries come to the city, including the beginning of the Sherwin-Williams paint business, and the automotive industry, all of which saw the massive increase in the city's population, which continued to grow through the 1950s.

But times would change in the ensuing decades. With the move to international manufacturing, the city began to see the closure of businesses starting in the 1970s. Companies such as U.S. Steel, which had been around since 1901, began to shut their doors, unable to compete with the lower costs of foreign companies.

WESTINGHOUSE ELECTRIC CORPORATION

Westinghouse first began in 1886 in Pittsburgh. They produced turbines, generators, motors, and switch gear, all for the use in the creation and transmission of electricity. Their major competitor was none other than Thomas Edison, whose company would go on to become known as General Electric.

Interestingly, Westinghouse moved to Cleveland only after a successful lawsuit against a different competitor which had infringed upon their patented process, and the company was ordered to be sold to Westinghouse in 1898. The company took over and began to expand, opening more factories in Cuyahoga County, including the Cedar Avenue complex.

The property began its life in 1888 as a power plant for the East Cleveland Railroad Company, used to operate their railcar lines via electricity. Upgrades to the engines and expansions to the building began as soon as the following year, and the company merged with another to form the Cleveland Electric Railway in 1893.

Four years later, even greater power was needed, and a new plant was completed in 1899, which featured one of the largest electric generators in the world at that time. By the following year, the plant had become the largest non-condensing, direct-current plant in the U.S.

1901 saw a battery storage facility built on the property and a coal handling device the following year to help unload the 60,000 tons of coal used per year at the plant. But even still, additional power was needed by the railways, and beginning in 1912, the company began to outsource its power generation. The company left power generation altogether in 1917, and the Cedar plant was reopened by Westinghouse and the Cleveland Ice Machine Company. Westinghouse used the plant to manufacture and sell a variety of products including circuit breakers, elevator motors and controls, lamps and light fixtures (used in airports and on highways), heaters, welding equipment, and switchboards.

The property was purchased in 1936 by Thompson Products, one of the nation's largest auto valve manufacturers. Like many companies, they moved into military applications with World War II and began producing valves for the military, including the U.S. Air Force. It is this division of the company which would move into the Cedar facility in 1941.

However, post-war saw a rapid decline in orders and the company began to downsize considerably, eventually moving most of its production to Euclid, Ohio, with only the Special Products Division, automotive replacement parts, and other various forged metal parts being produced at the Cleveland plant. Thompson Products merged with Ramo-Wooldridge, a weapon systems manufacturer which focused on guided missiles, becoming the Thompson-Ramo-Wooldridge Company. The Cedar facility now became a part of the company's Light Metals division before selling the building in 1962 and moving elsewhere.

The following year, the facility opened as an addition to the Virden Company, a metal manufacturer focusing on brass and electroplating, which had seen a boom in orders in the 1960s. But the following decade saw a drop in the housing market, for which Virden produced lighting fixtures. The company downsized over the decade before finally closing in 1980 after being unable to pay its employees. That same year, an auction was held selling off all machinery and the property. The plant has remained abandoned since, being used for two scenes in 2012's *The Avengers*, which utilized the railway station, as well as first and second stories of the plant for scenes.

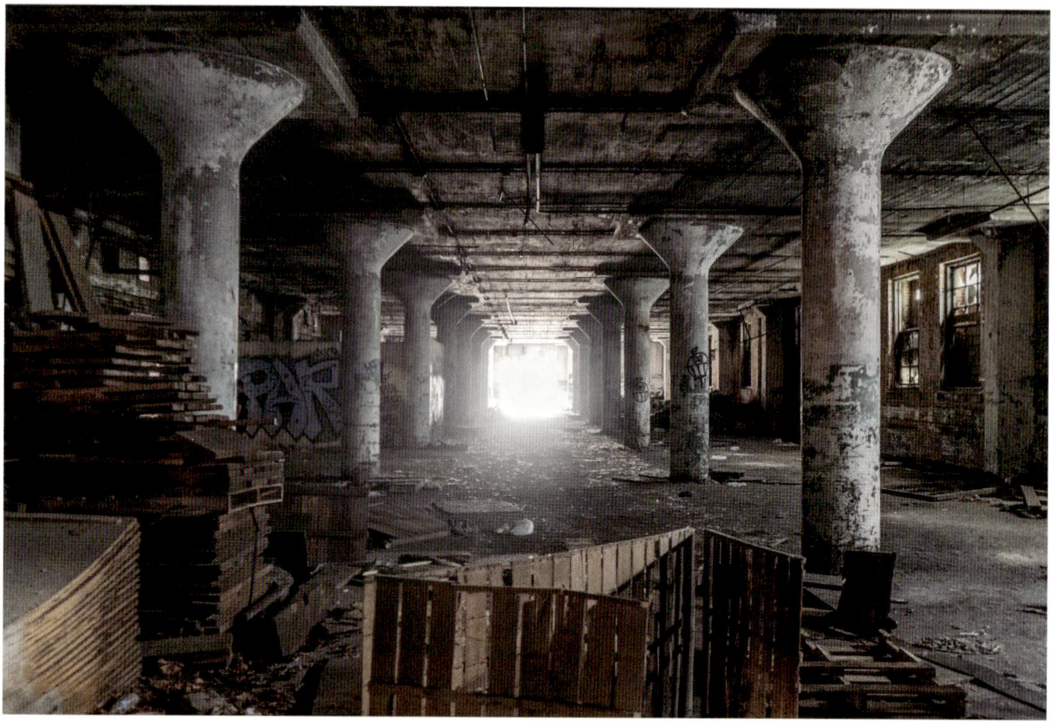

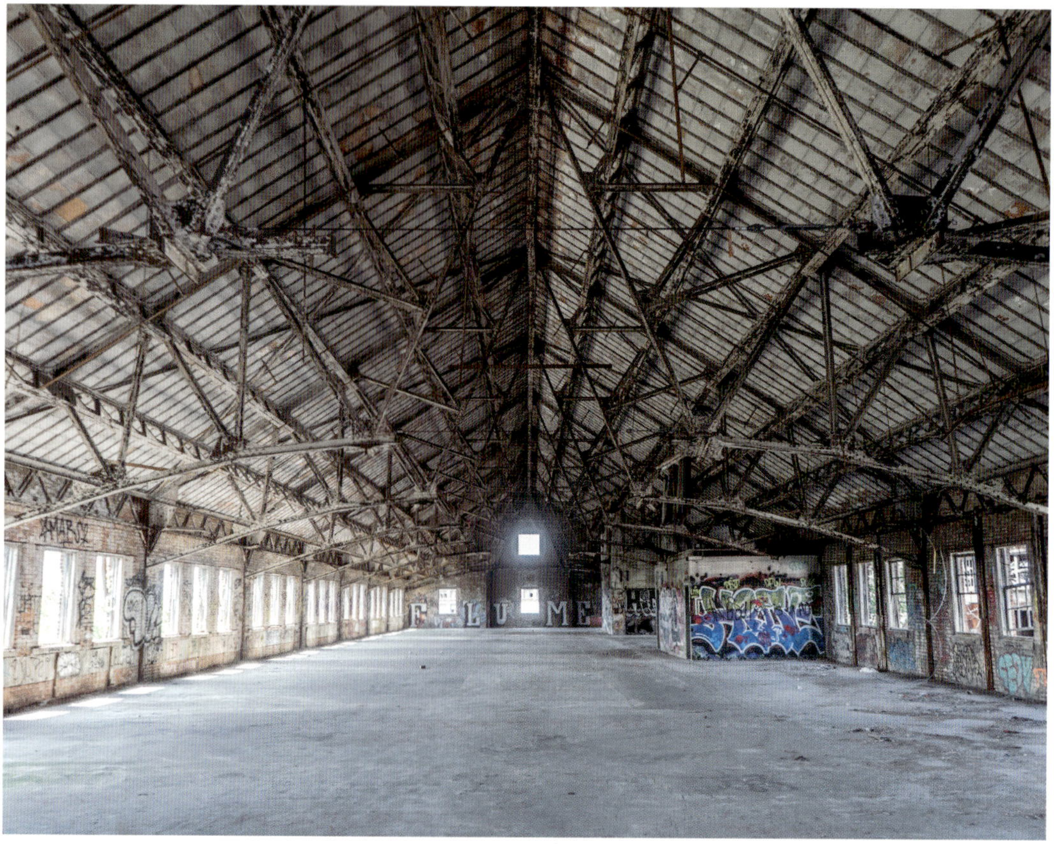
FLUME

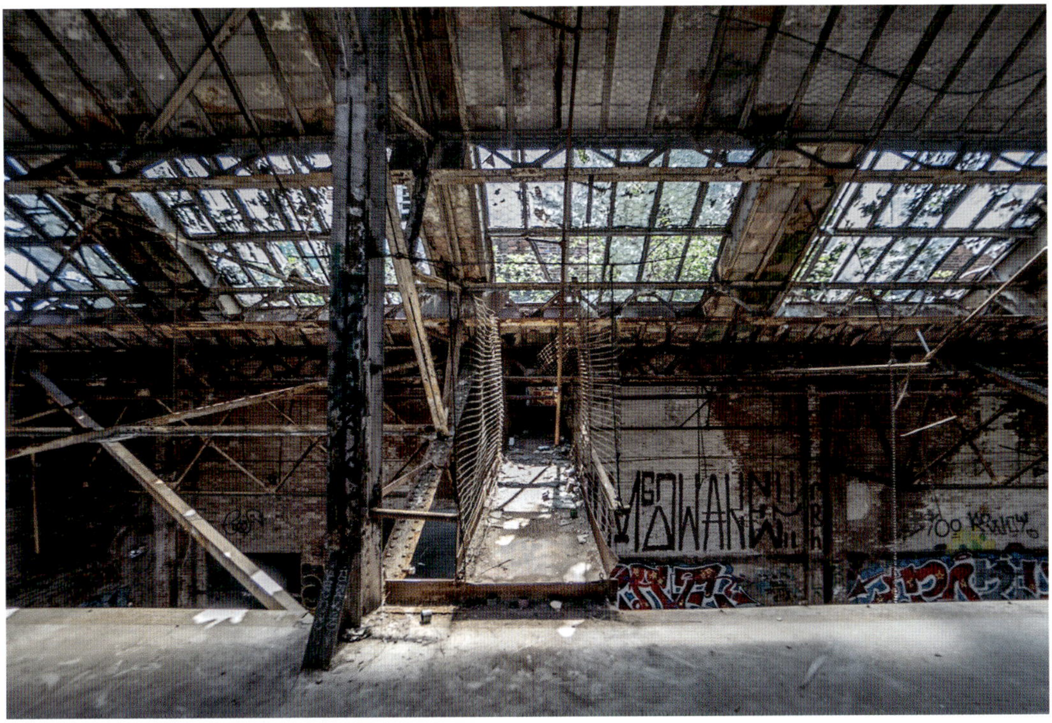

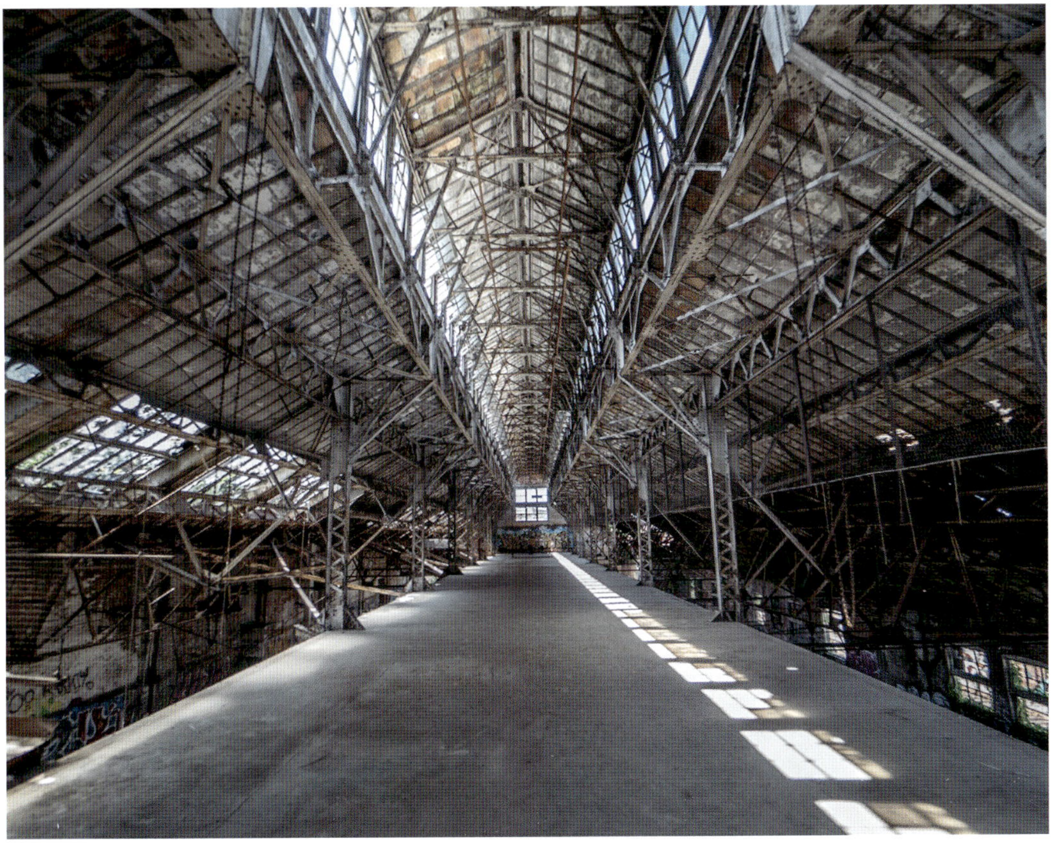

WARNER AND SWASEY COMPANY

Not far up the railways from the Westinghouse factory lay the five-story remains of the Warner and Swasey Co., a machine tool manufacturer that specialized in telescopes and precision instruments. The company was formed in 1880 by Worchester P. Warner and Ambrose Swasey in Chicago before moving the following year to Cleveland in order to be closer to the businesses for which they supplied turret lathes.

They began to produce telescopes soon thereafter and, in 1886, became known for creating the largest telescope in the world. Although they are most remembered for the telescopes they created, it is their lathes which kept them in business, and by 1928, they had become the leading producer in the world. With such booming business, a new building was needed to replace the original 1881 building. Over the course of six years, beginning in 1904, the current factory building was constructed on the property.

During World War I, the company provided parts for tommy guns. By the time World War II broke, they employed 7,000 workers, producing parts for airplanes, tanks, and ships. Post-war, the company moved into construction equipment for textile machinery, as well as electronics.

As with many other companies at the time, they began to leave Cleveland in the 1960s, and their employment sank to 2,000. They were acquired by Bendix Corporation in 1980 and the Cleveland factory was closed just five years later. The company itself remained in business a little longer, finally closing in 1992.

The city of Cleveland purchased the original property the year prior, demolishing a small section, where they have since constructed a garage for city vehicles. The remaining building has sat abandoned since, with the city attempting to redevelop or demolish it multiple times to no avail.

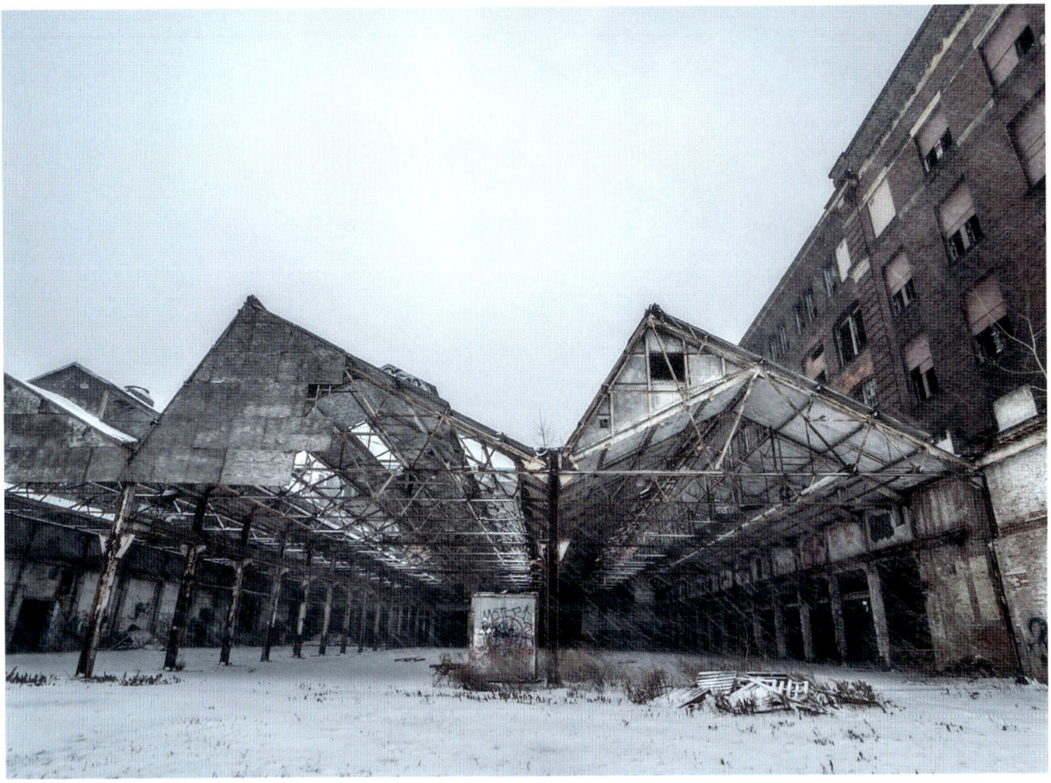

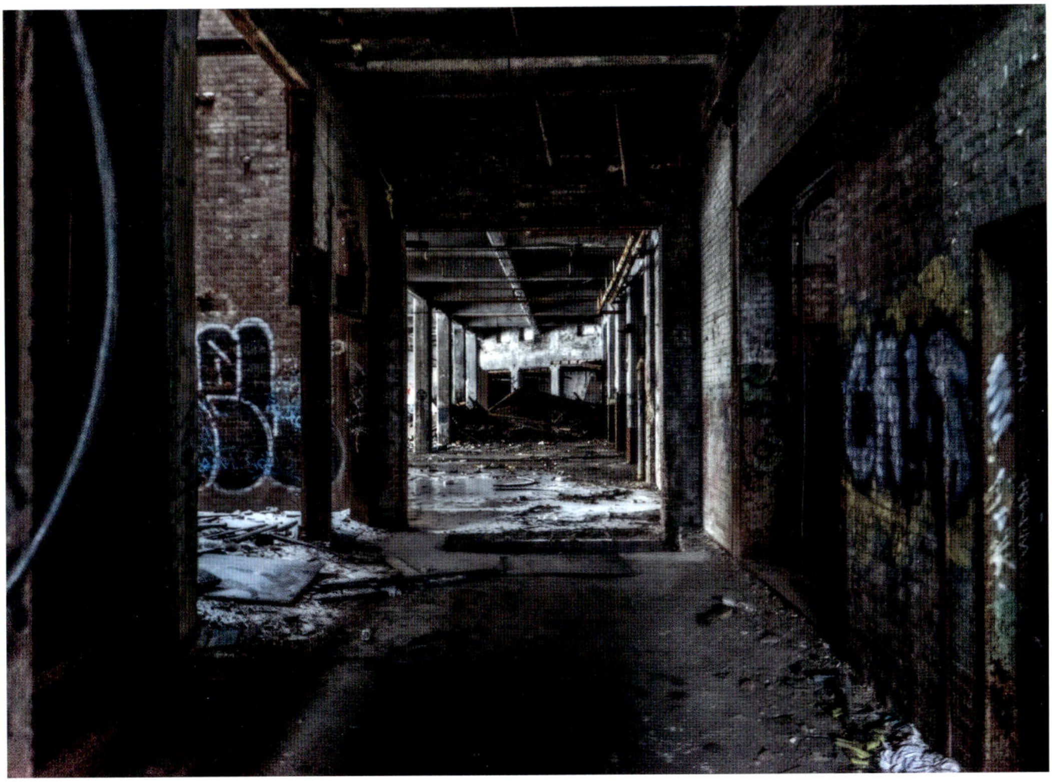

NATIONAL ACME COMPANY

In 1895, the Acme Screw Machine Company began in Connecticut, producing lathe machines. The company began to struggle in a few years and looked at partnerships with manufacturing companies in Cleveland. In 1901, Acme merged with the National Manufacturing Company and moved all operations to the city, becoming the National Acme Manufacturing Company, producing automated machine tools, foundry equipment, and electrical controls.

The company grew to become one of the city's largest manufacturers, completing their new factory in 1916. The following decades saw the company acquire several other businesses across the nation and world, eventually merging with the Cleveland Twist Drill Company in 1968. Together, the pair would become the Acme-Cleveland Corporation to produce similar machine tools for metal foundries.

From 1980 to 1982, National Acme had annual sales exceeding $400 million, making them one of the largest machine-tool manufacturers in America. The following year would see a nearly $32 million loss with the increasing global marketplace competition. Combined with a nationwide recession, the business began to downsize, operating just the National Acme and Cleveland Twist Drill factories in the city.

To stay afloat, the company diversified by moving into the telecommunications market. They continued to move further into electrical manufacturing in the 1990s and further downsized their metalworking, selling the Cleveland Twist Drill building in 1994 and National Acme the following year. It was purchased by a similar machine tool manufacturer until going bankrupt in 1999. It was next used as rentable storage space, though few companies utilized it, as it had become a high-crime neighborhood.

The property would eventually be used by a garbage disposal company in 2011 as a cardboard and paper waste recycling center. The owners were given prison sentences after it was determined they improperly demolished sections of the factory, releasing asbestos into the air while filling the remainder of the building with trash.

The court case ruled the owners pay for the cleanup and demolition of the remaining buildings, which will cost roughly six million, a debt they know is highly unlikely they will ever collect. Today, the building remains abandoned, with around 40,000 tons of refuse rotting inside.

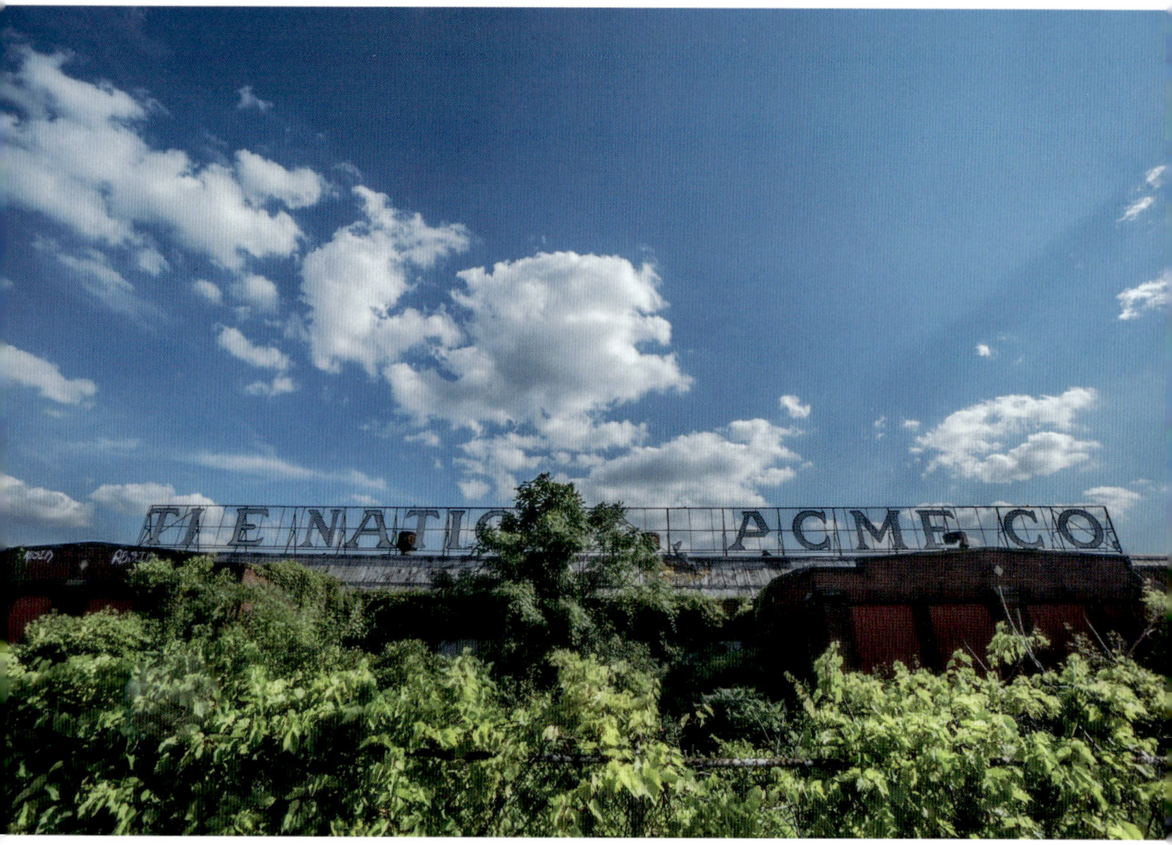
ACME CO

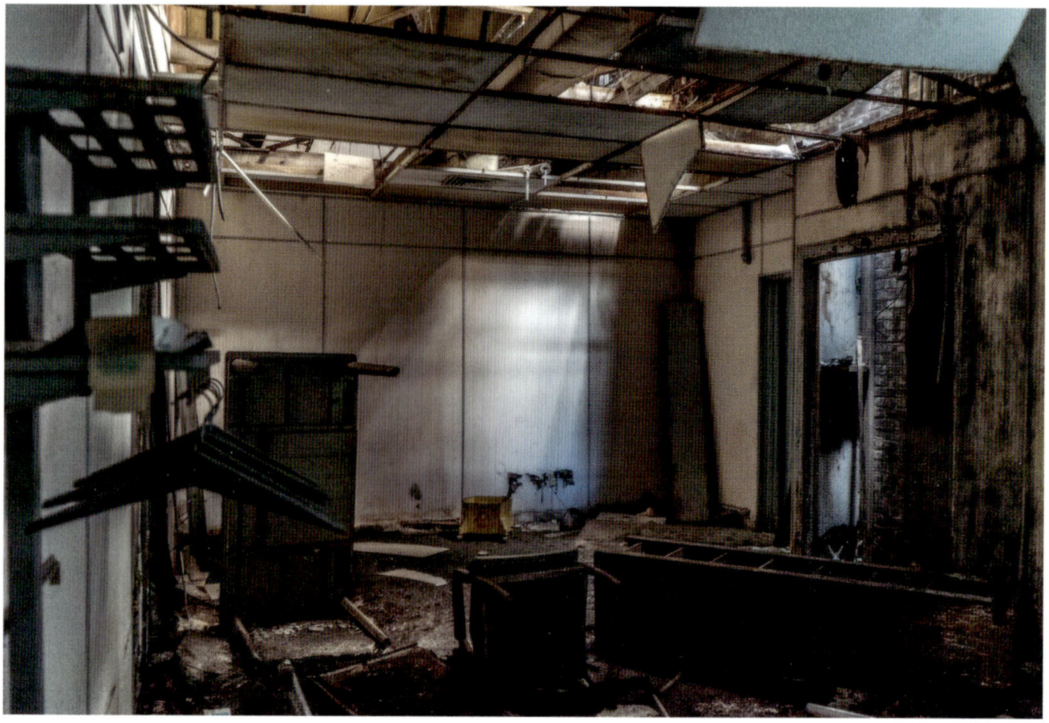

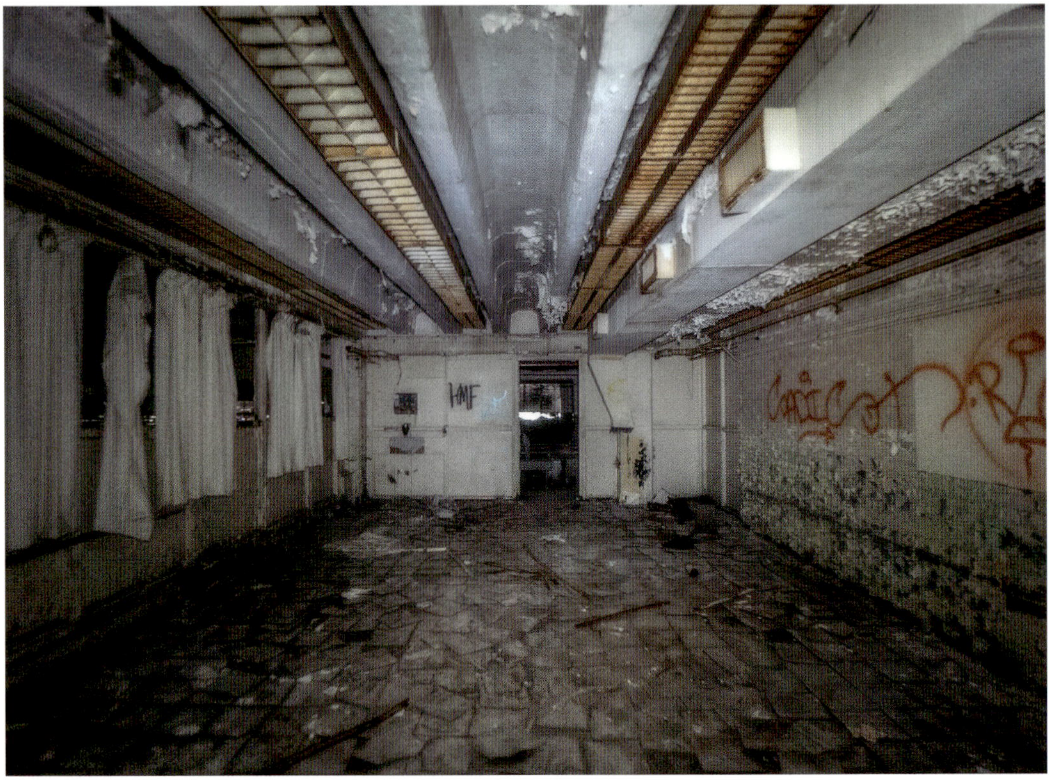

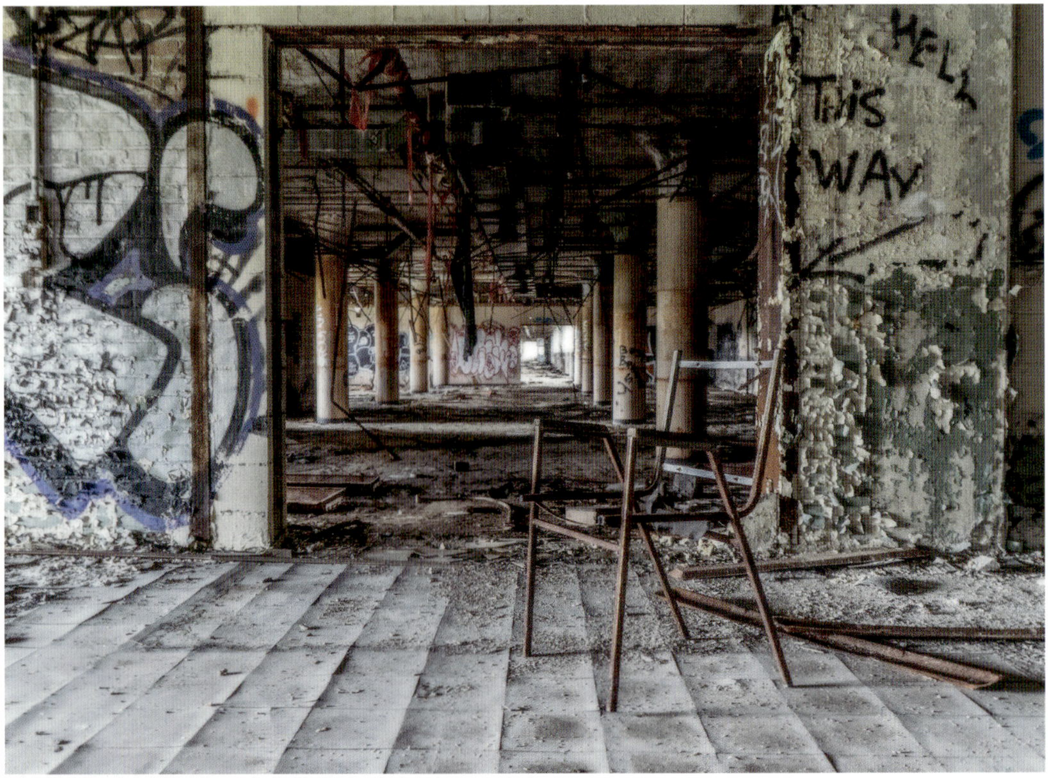
HELL
THIS
WAY

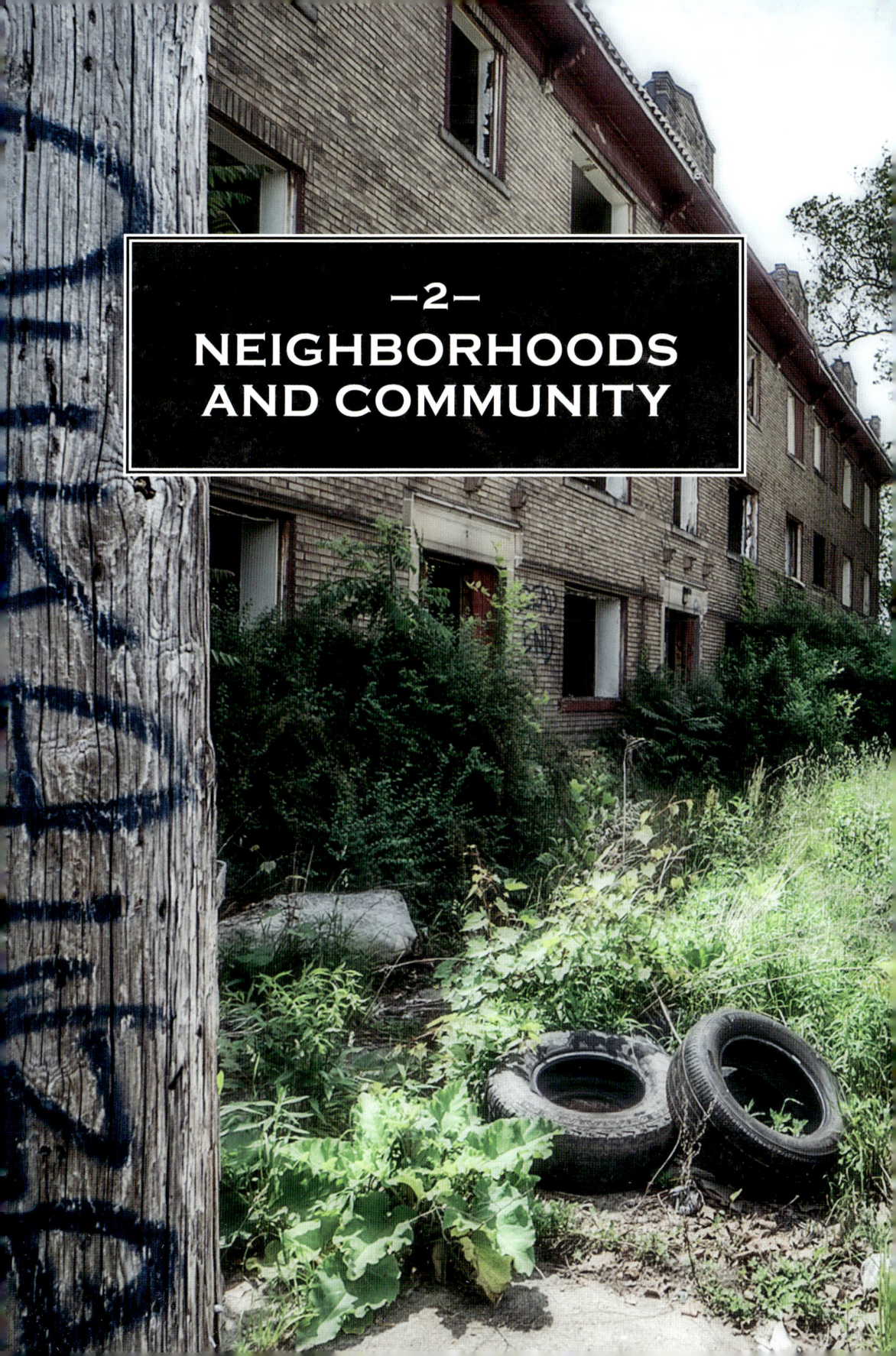

–2–
NEIGHBORHOODS AND COMMUNITY

The start of the new millennium found an ideal market for both first-time homeowners as well as current owners, due to the low mortgage interest rates and a high approval rate for loans. With this easy money, many could now purchase homes that were otherwise outside of their means. Beginning in 2006, however, the rug was pulled out from under these owners when interest rates began to increase again. Many found they could no longer afford the higher rates, leading to a high foreclosure rate.

This mortgage crisis affected the entire United States, but its effects were particularly hard-hitting in larger cities such as Cleveland and Detroit. The first three months of the crisis saw a total of 783 foreclosures in Cleveland alone. Unable to pay for their homes, many residents simply walked away from them, leaving the houses open to squatters, scrappers, and vandals. These blighted properties in turn decreased the value of the homes around them, which led to the homeowners or landlords to neglect upkeep on their own properties that had a decreased value. Homes that would sell for $80,000 were now plummeting to a mere $18,000.

By the time the crisis had ended around 2010, Cuyahoga County had roughly 22,000 vacant homes. Four years later, that number remained largely unchanged. Some of the hardest-hit neighborhoods remain today with a staggering rate upwards of sixteen percent unoccupied homes. Both the city and volunteer organizations have fought valiantly at demolishing the more distressed properties, a process which came to be recognized as one of the forefront in the nation.

But at an approximate cost of $10,000 per demolition, it is a battle that is far from over. Banks are still hesitant to give loans to inner-city residents, with some neighborhoods on a point-blank rejection list. Furthermore, a new problem has risen from the mass demolitions: rodents. After the home they were nesting in is demolished, mice, rats, possums, and even coyotes have been reported taking residence in the nearby homes. Nearly a decade after the crisis ended, the city is still losing its residents, with 4,500 moving elsewhere in 2018 alone.

ELDERWOOD

The once-vibrant city of East Cleveland is home to General Electric's lighting division. A stretch of four miles along Euclid Avenue was referred to as Millionaire's Row. Its lavish mansions were home to some of the nation's elite, including John D. Rockefeller. But less than four miles down the same road sits the almost completely abandoned neighborhood of Elderwood.

This middle-class neighborhood was largely made up of more than fifteen apartment buildings as well as single-family homes, much of which sprung up in 1920. Many of the occupants worked at the GE plant, which was close enough for them to walk to during the warmer months. The neighborhood would eventually go downhill in the 1980s, when the city was in the midst of a crack epidemic, and reports mention the area around Elderwood were rife with drugs and murder.

This section of Elderwood was also home to future serial killer Anthony Sowell, who lived there from 1985 to 1990, before being arrested for raping a woman at his home, choking her to the point she believed she would die. Incidentally, a string of murders taking place nearby would cease after Sowell was jailed, a story we will be covering in Chapter 5.

At some point in the 1990s, a fire would break out on the street, which caused the death of several residents, including children, and is the main citation for the mass abandonment of the neighborhood. Since then, this section of Elderwood and its cross streets have remained largely vacant, lending to a string of crimes occurring ever since.

In 2004, the body of a woman was found in a group of bushes along the street, the leather belt she was strangled with left wrapped around her throat—a crime later linked to a convicted sex offender. A man living in one of the few occupied apartments would testify he witnessed a robbery-turned-murder a block north of Elderwood in 2011, as well as the fatal shooting of a high school student in the street outside his home. A string of arson fires hit the neighborhood in 2013, and that same year search teams would discover what was believed to be a human bone in one vacant apartment after another nearby serial killer was apprehended, a story which will also be covered later.

In recent years, some buildings have been purchased with plans to be renovated, but they largely remain vacant; the city is instead utilizing its inadequate demolition funds to remove blight in more lived-in neighborhoods. Until then, the problems will remain in Elderwood. State investigators executed search warrants on a business in the neighborhood in connection with an environmental contamination case taking place at a dump site in the city in 2017.

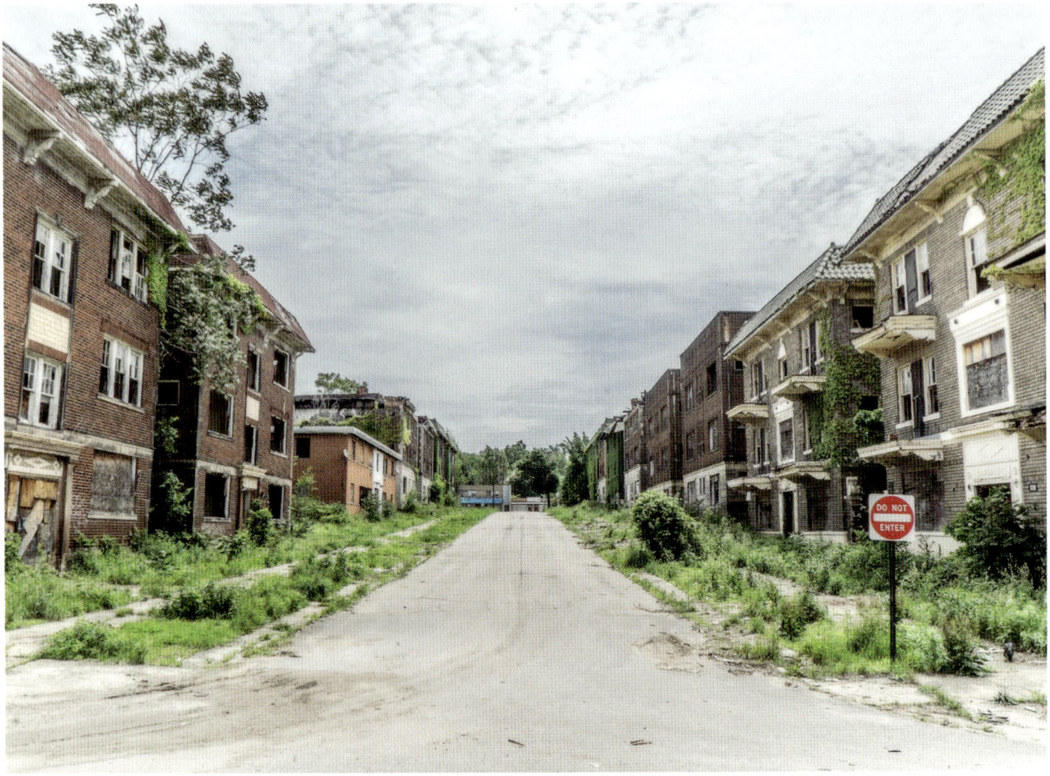
DO NOT
ENTER

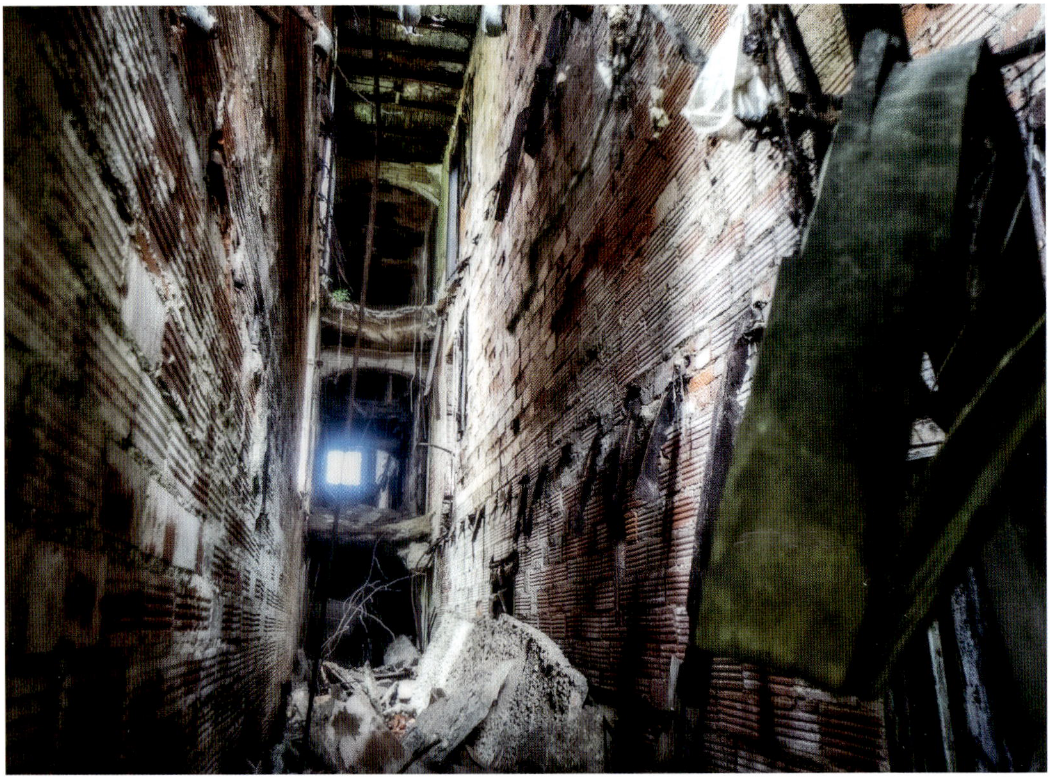

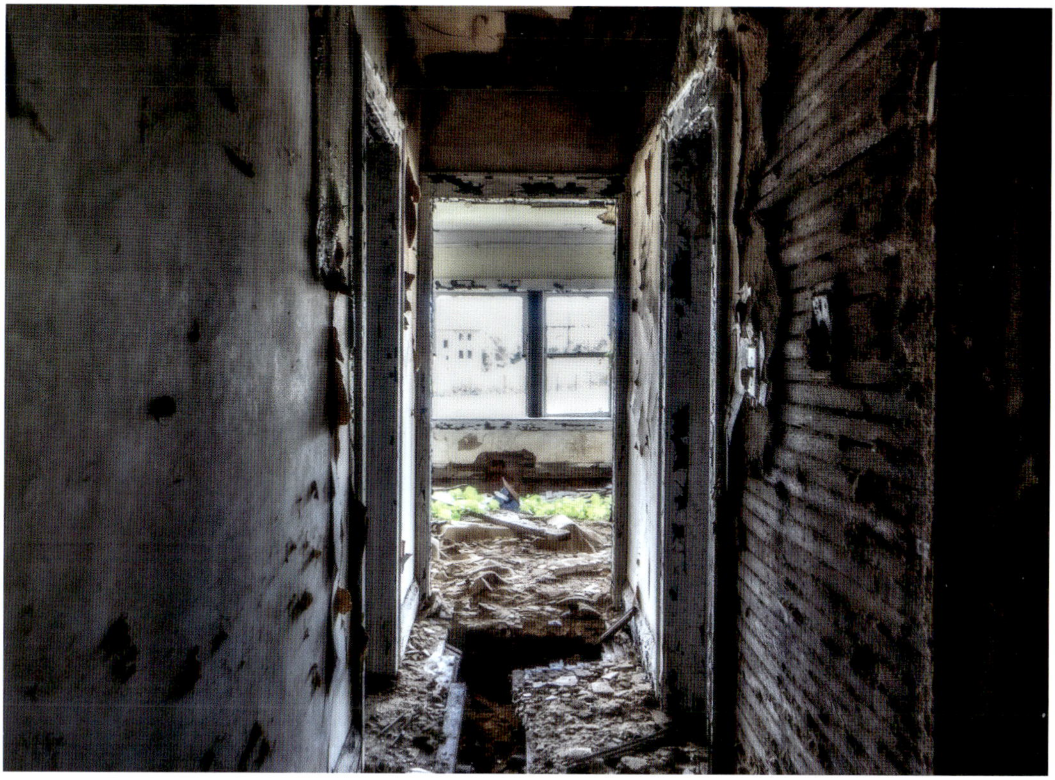

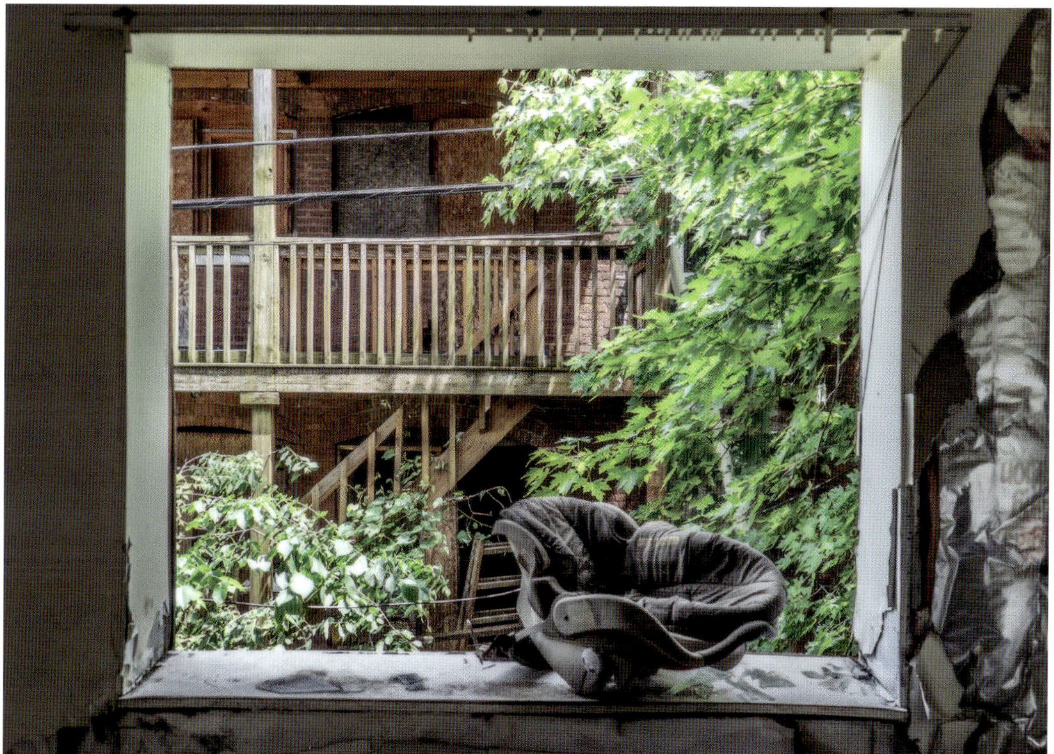

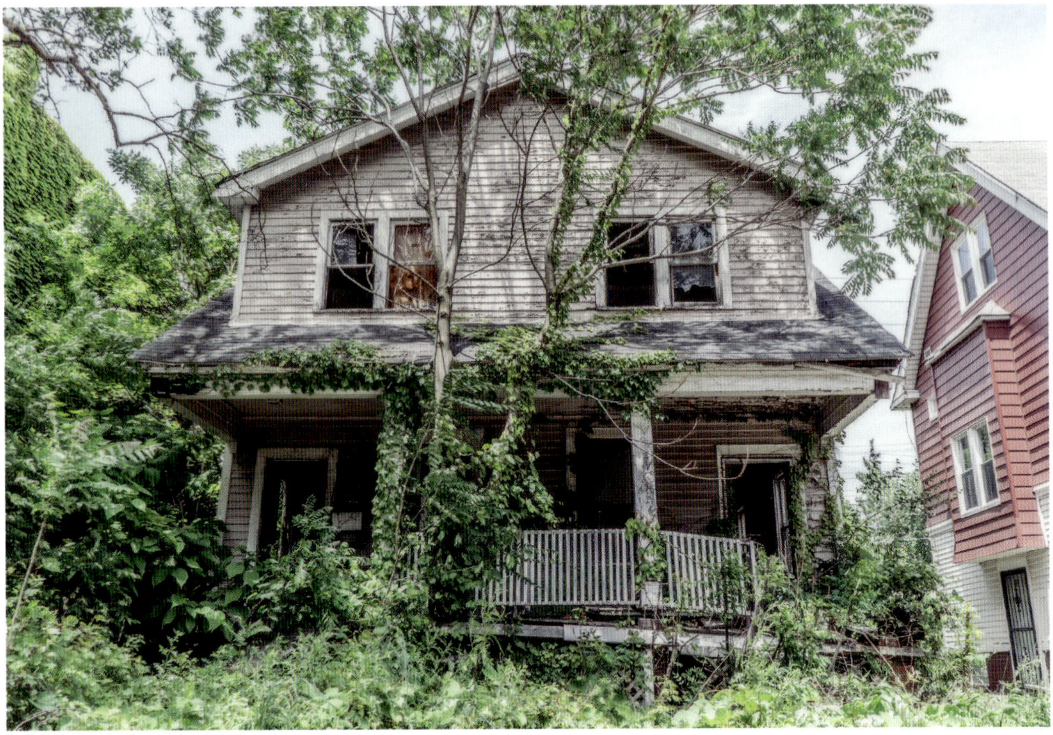

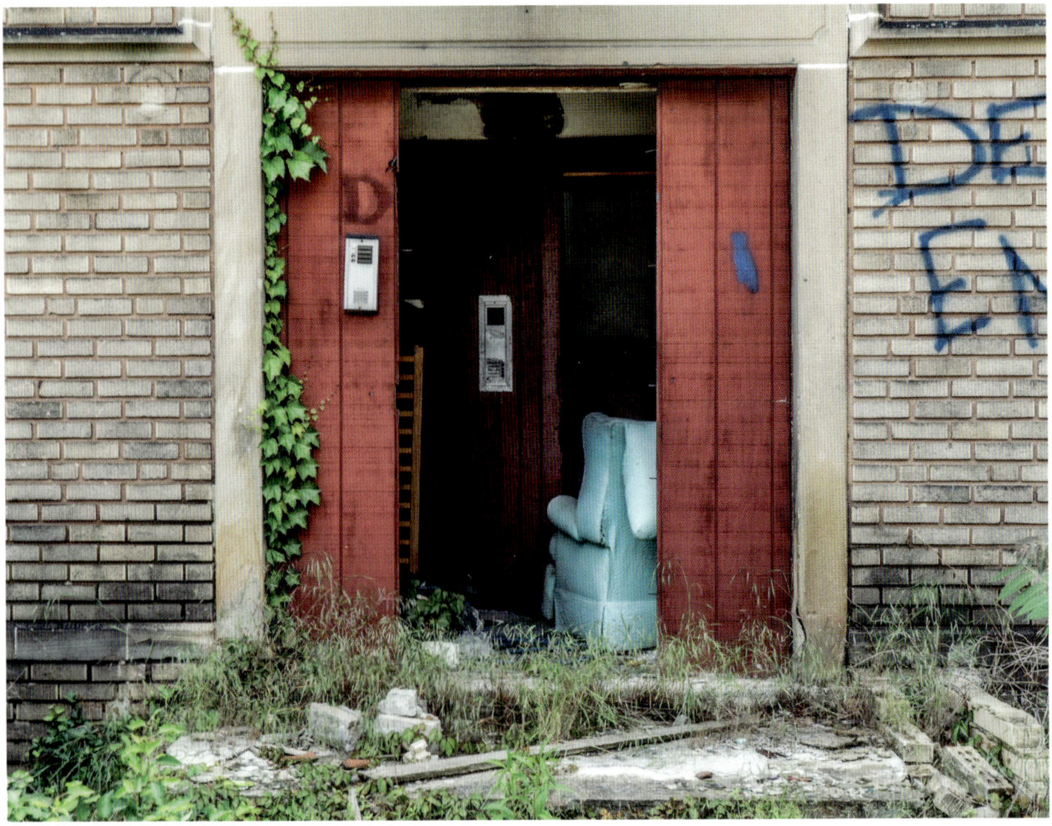

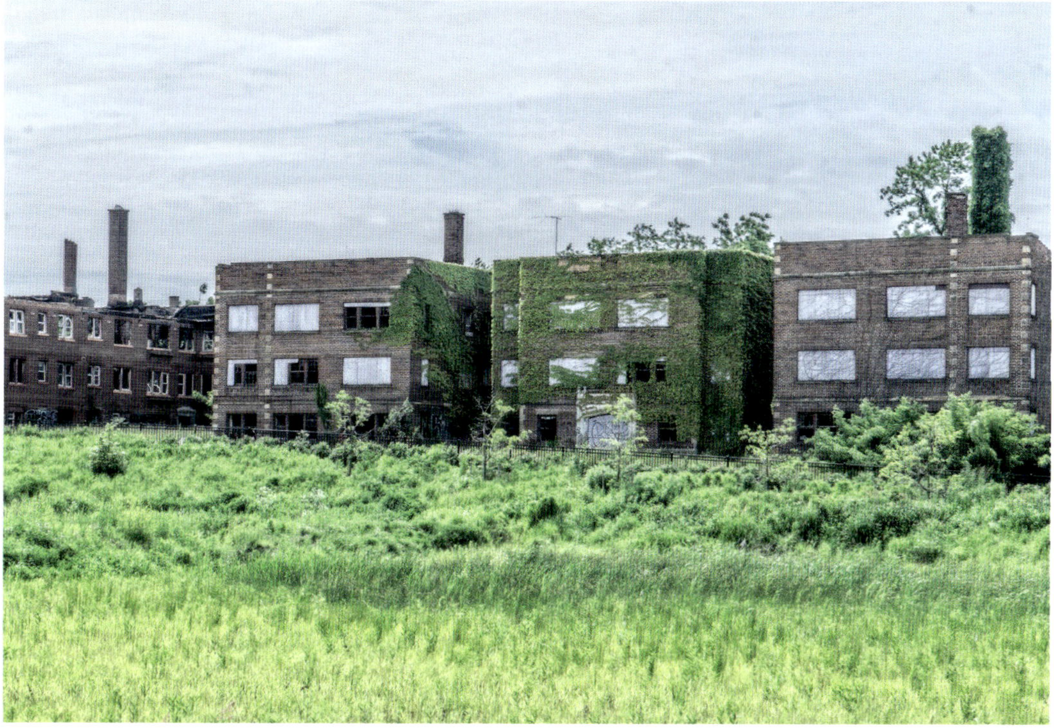

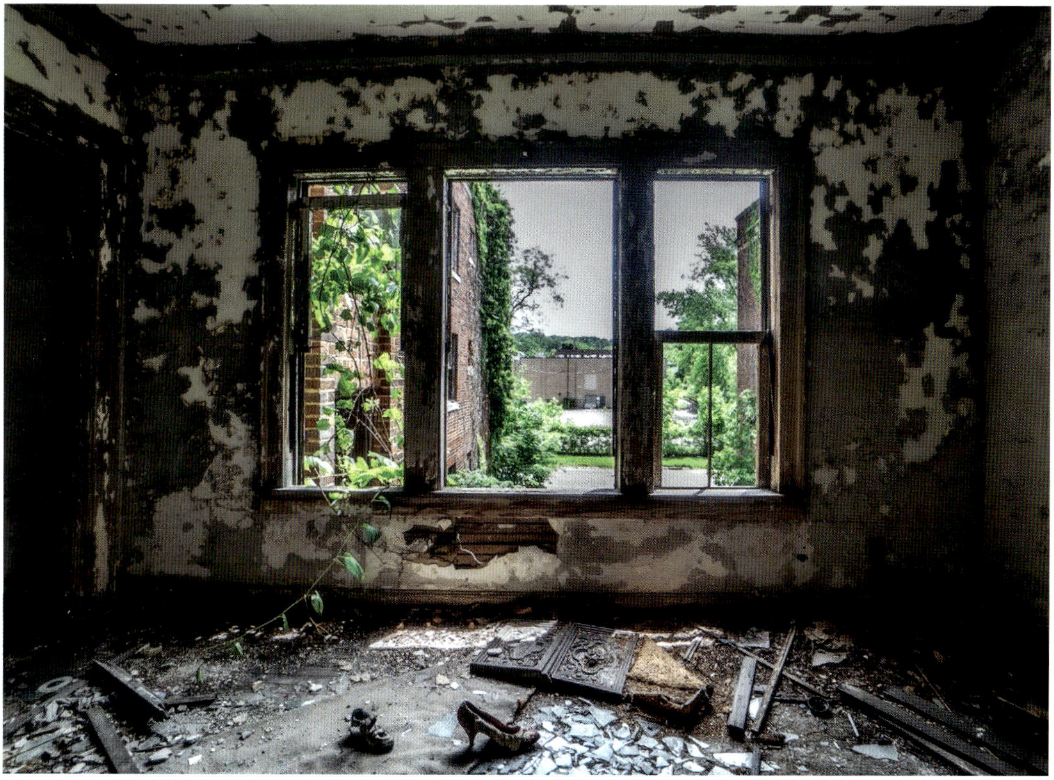

SLAVIC VILLAGE

Before becoming its own community, Slavic Village was a part of one of Cuyahoga County's oldest settlements, Newburgh. Like much of the rest of Cleveland, Slavic Village saw its growth and industrialization with the creation of the Ohio & Erie Canal. Immigrants to the neighborhood were primarily from Czechoslovakia, Poland, and Slovakia, who brought with them their culture and religion, founding churches and halls, many of which remain today.

By the 1920s, Broadway Avenue, which runs through the heart of Slavic Village, is noted as rivaling the downtown in terms of commercial development. A primarily working-class neighborhood, most worked in the nearby factories; however, some operated their own businesses in the neighborhoods. Fleet Avenue in particular was dominated by local Polish-owned businesses. The population reached its peak in 1940, with more than 68,000 residents.

That number would drop to less than half that by the millennium, and the impending foreclosure crisis only made matters worse. Slavic Village was the worst-hit neighborhood in the city that became known for having the most foreclosures in the country. One in eleven houses were abandoned, and Broadway Avenue, which rivaled downtown, became largely empty.

But through it all, the Slavic Village Development (SVD) has worked to fix up or demolish blighted properties. More than $200 million was invested into the community, bringing businesses such as the headquarters of the Third Federal Bank, as well as the Cleveland Velodrome, one of only a handful of Fast Track Cycle facilities in the country.

Things were looking up for the community, but then a rash of brutal crime reminded residents and politicians that things were still far from okay. A twelve-year-old died by a stray bullet from a shootout between two drug addicts; another man was shot in the face while working in his driveway. A spate of robberies resulted in at least four deaths of elderly residents in their homes. Two deaths and a burglary all occurred in the span of just one week in 2018. Violent crime rose 76 percent from 1990, and drug arrests have quadrupled, leading to the FBI to lend a hand.

Much of Slavic Village remains abandoned, but with the continued efforts of the SVD, along with neighborhood block groups, the community is working on continuing to turn things around for the neighborhood.

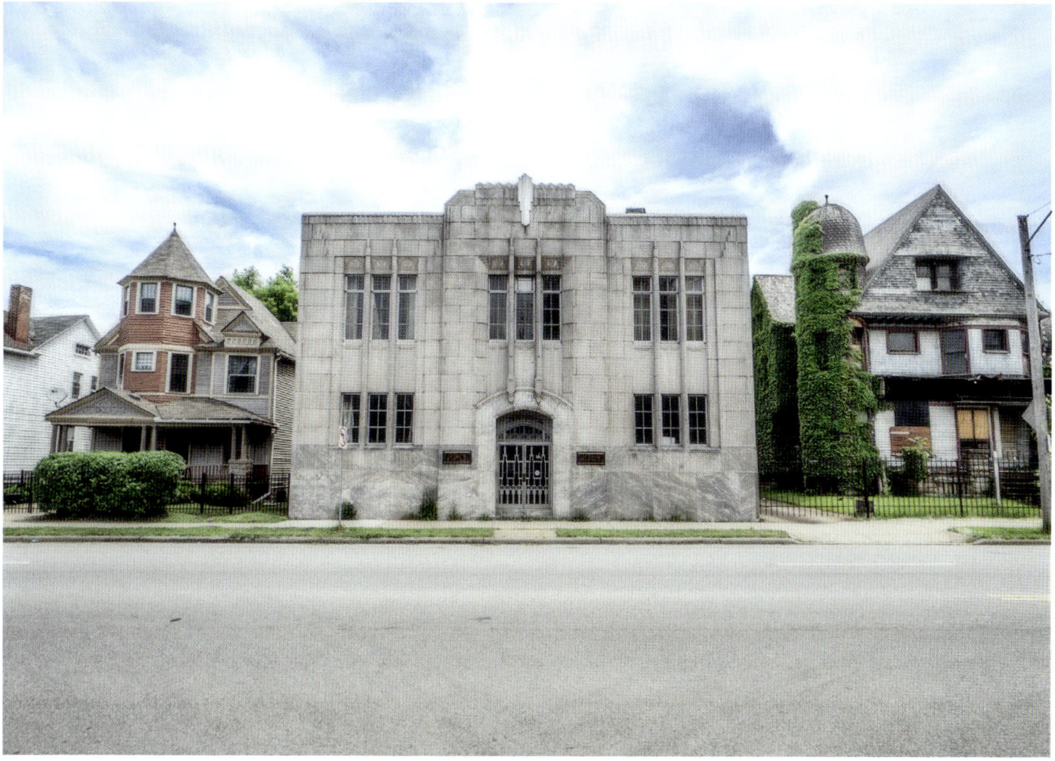

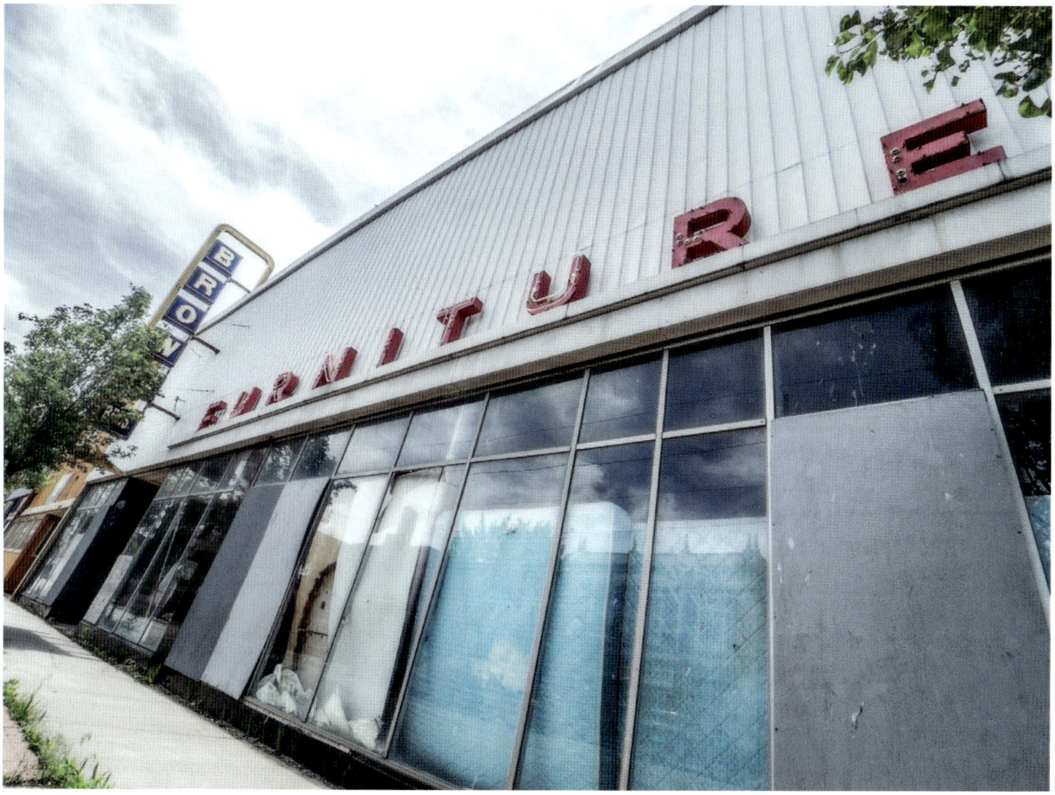
BROW
FURNITURE

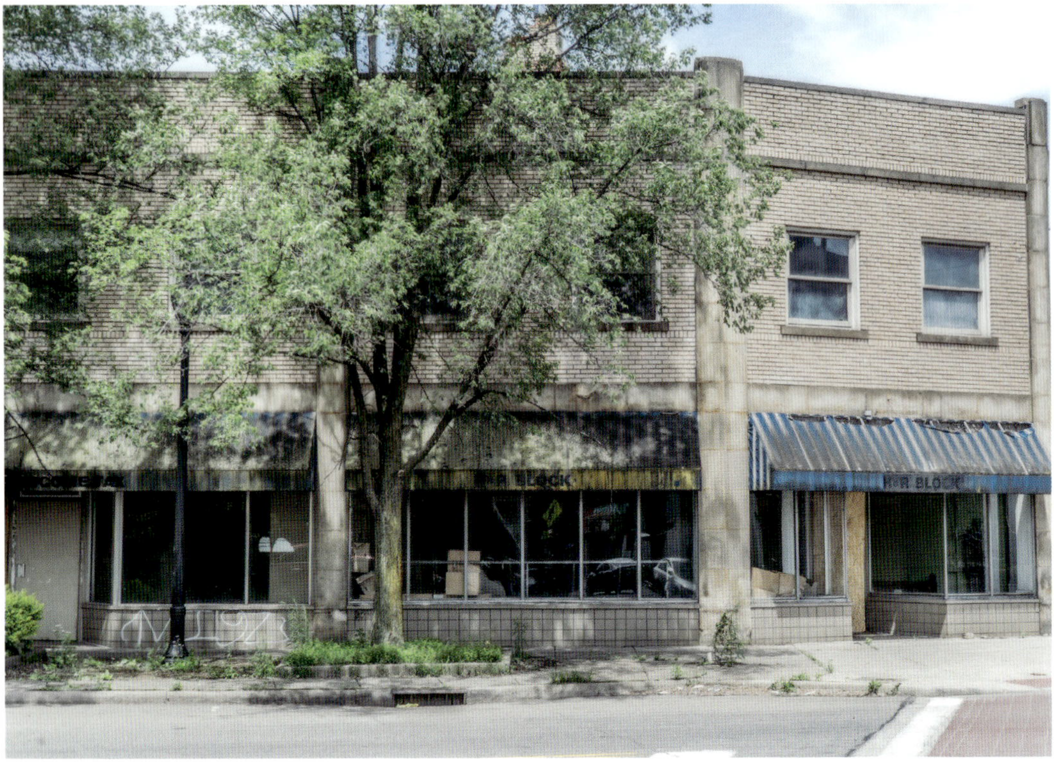

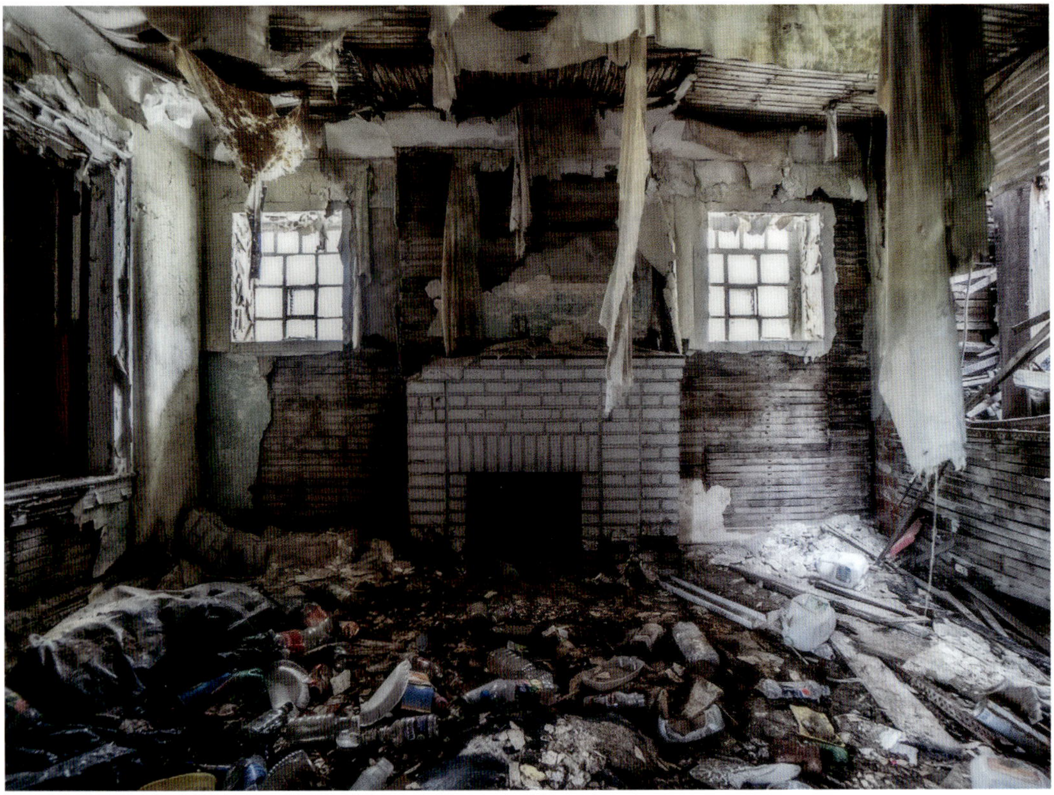

Above left: House of Our Redeemer Church.

SIDAWAY BRIDGE

The first bridge built to connect the primarily Hungarian Kinsman Road neighborhood with the largely Polish Jackowo neighborhood was built in 1909. This pedestrian footbridge spanning the Kingsbury Run ravine was the longest wooden bridge ever built in Cleveland at 675 feet long and a height of eighty feet. Originally named the Tod-Kinsman Bridge, it was meant to help bring the two neighborhoods together, which had been experiencing tensions.

The area below the bridge was eyed by the Nickel Plate Railroad Company in the late 1920s as a location to build several train car barns; however, the bridge was in the way. An agreement between the railroad and the city saw the company construct a new suspension bridge in its place in 1930, the only bridge of its kind in Cleveland.

Just five years after opening, the area became the dumping ground for the "Mad Butcher of Kingsbury Run," who murdered at least twelve women between 1935 and 1938, dumping four of those bodies off the side of the bridge. The killer, who later became known as the "Cleveland Torso Murderer," was never caught, but his idea stuck. Another murdered woman was dumped off the bridge in the early 1960s.

That same decade saw an increase in racial tensions. As the Kinsman neighborhood began to shift to African American, their children would use the bridge to walk to their school in the Jackowo neighborhood, to the disapproval of that neighborhood's residents. Tensions came to a head in 1966 with the Hough riots when the bridge had portions of its wooden floor removed and was attempted to be burned down. Rather than repair it, the city decided to abandon the bridge, a decision later cited as part of their plan to continue segregation by a federal judge.

Renovations to the bridge have been mentioned multiple times in recent decades, but it has remained abandoned.

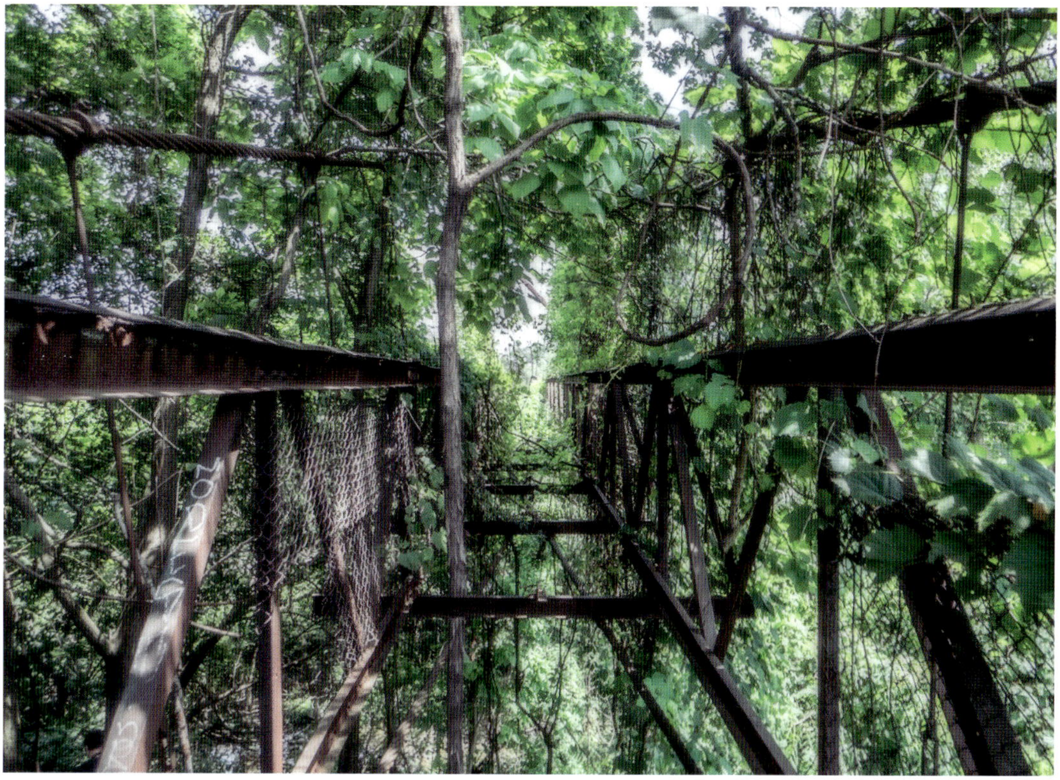

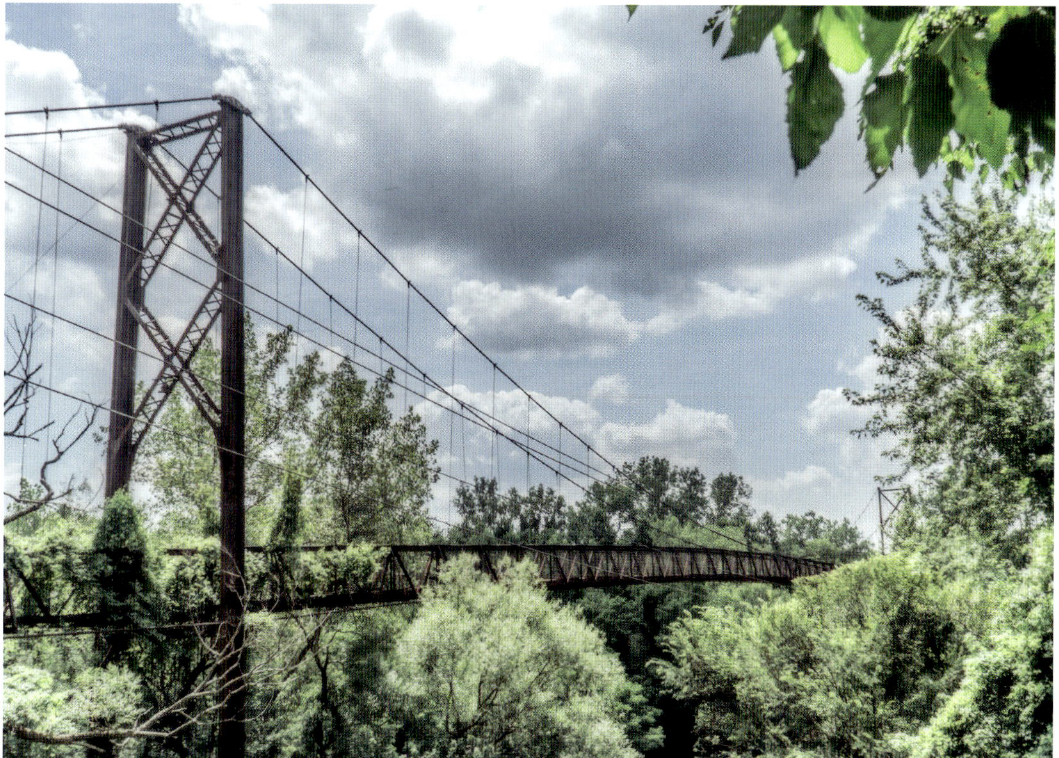

—3—
SCHOOLS

C leveland's first public school opened in 1836, with two separate private schools having been in the area up to two decades earlier. Additional schools were constructed to meet the needs of the growing population, including teaching English and civics classes for the numerous immigrants moving to the city. Other instances of adaptation to the area included industrial training in the public schools, since many of their graduates would go on to work in the local factories.

In 1908, a fire broke out in one of the city's elementary schools, killing 172 students, raising complaints of overcrowding in a school system which had seen rapid growth—64,409 students attended the Cleveland Metropolitan School District in 1912, and that number had soared to over 100,000 within the next six years, along with many more attending academies and private schools. At its height in 1963, CMSD had nearly 150,000 students enrolled.

But even before that number would drop considerably in the 1970s, the school system faced difficulties, with more than half of its 174 schools terribly outdated, having been built more than fifty years earlier. Cleveland also ranked as the lowest pupil expenditure rate in all of Cuyahoga County in the 1960s. About 14,000 students were forced to attend school for only half of the day in 1960, as there were not enough teachers or classrooms for all to attend, and the problems would only grow larger with the decreased tax revenue as the result of "white flight" and the increased population shift to the suburbs.

The problems would continue into the 1980s, when only thirty-seven percent of adults in the city had graduated from high school, and it was estimated that there were 47,000 residents who could be considered illiterate. The 1990s were no better, with almost half of students failing to graduate high school, and of those that did, many still did not qualify for entry-level jobs. In 2009, Cleveland had the third-highest dropout rate in the nation.

Regardless of the decreased revenue and drop in enrollment, CMSD did not close schools, or make the proper budget cuts until after the millennium, despite in 1993 the state's superintendent estimating a $55 million deficit that same year, and a doubling of that amount the following year. Cleveland was given a $75 million emergency loan, though it retained ownership of the school buildings.

Finally, beginning in 2005, CMSD began to seriously reform and reorganize, closing thirty-five schools over the next decade. Today, the system is continuing to make strides to correct itself, but much remains to be done. The enrollment rate is a shadow of what it once was, with only 38,949 students in 2019, and an additional four schools marked for closure. Of these closed schools, few have been purchased by outside parties, and less than half have been demolished—the required funds reaching upward of $2 million for some buildings hard to come by.

PRECIOUS LITTLE PEOPLE DAYCARE

Little is known about this building; it was constructed in 1955 and used by the Steelblast Abrasive Company until 1975. They manufactured artificial abrasives used in polishing, grinding, and finishing surfaces of metal, wood, stone, and other materials.

In 2001, the property was purchased by Precious Little People Inc., an early childhood education center, teaching children ages six to twelve. The daycare abandoned the property around 2014 and neglected to secure it or pay taxes on it. At the time of writing, they owe almost $120,000 in back taxes to the city.

Just over a week after these photos were taken, a thrift store on the other side of the city was robbed at gunpoint. The two masked gunmen made off with an assortment of clothing including fifty pairs of Victoria's Secret leggings, fur coats, shoes, as well as cash and a store employee's cellphone and car keys. After paying two passersby $10 each to help load the car, they fled the scene. The following day, the abandoned car was discovered outside Precious Little People.

Buckeye-Woodland Elementary

Buckeye-Woodland Elementary School was constructed in 1975 with a modern, interior courtyard centered around the classrooms. A gymnasium, kitchen, and audio/visual classrooms were all added, branching off the main building the same year. Teaching kindergarten through sixth grade, it had a capacity of 358 students.

The school dealt with overcrowding, with roughly 500 students in 1988, but that number would drop to less than 300 post-millennium, despite the additions of seventh- and eighth-grade classes. An assessment of the building reported that while it was structurally sound, there was inadequate parking for cars and buses, no handicap accessibility, poor ventilation, unsecure playground areas, as well as recommended asbestos removal. Estimates for repairs and renovations totaled $881,621.40.

The school system did not act on any of these suggestions, and Buckeye-Woodland was ranked in the bottom half of all Cleveland Public Schools for overall test scores. Seeing their government was unwilling to help, the community stepped up and, in 2013, the Cleveland Browns organization and United Way volunteered to help build a fence and new playground, with players from the football team helping in the construction themselves. The following year, backpacks were donated by a nearby church, volunteers from the Jewish Cleveland organization read to students, and rapper K-Drama visited the school to show students how he created his music beats and performed a show.

Despite this outpouring for the school, it was one of sixteen buildings approved for closure by CMSD, shutting its doors for good in 2015. Demolition was approved in 2018, but no work was done. The following summer, CMSD found itself under fire when a news report revealed thousands of dollars' worth of educational material was left to rot inside the school. In response, every vacant school in Cleveland was re-secured, though many were done haphazardly and open within weeks to vandals and scrappers.

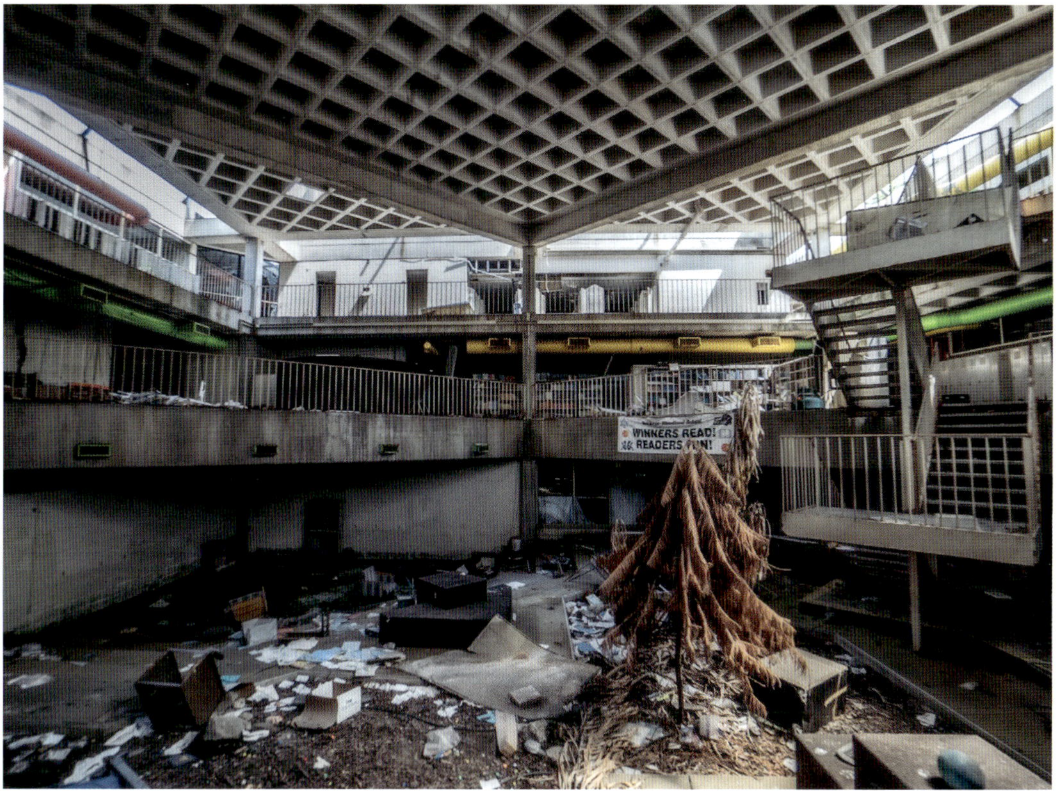
WINNERS READ!
READERS WIN!

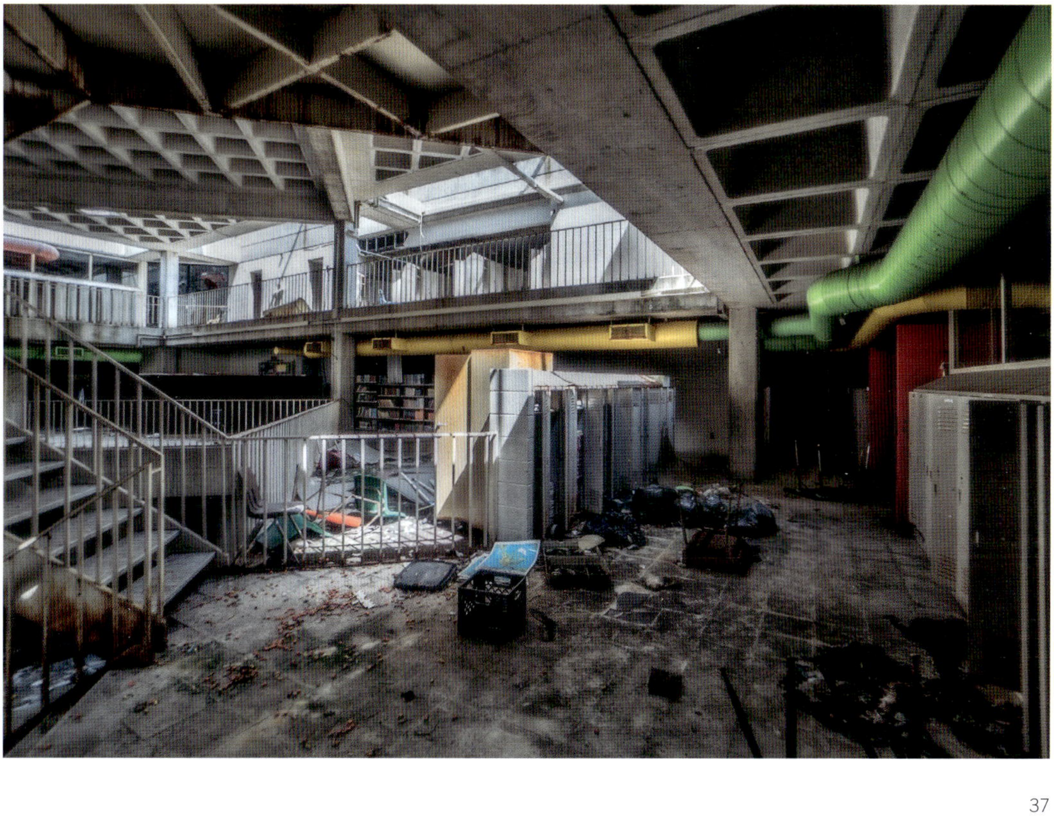

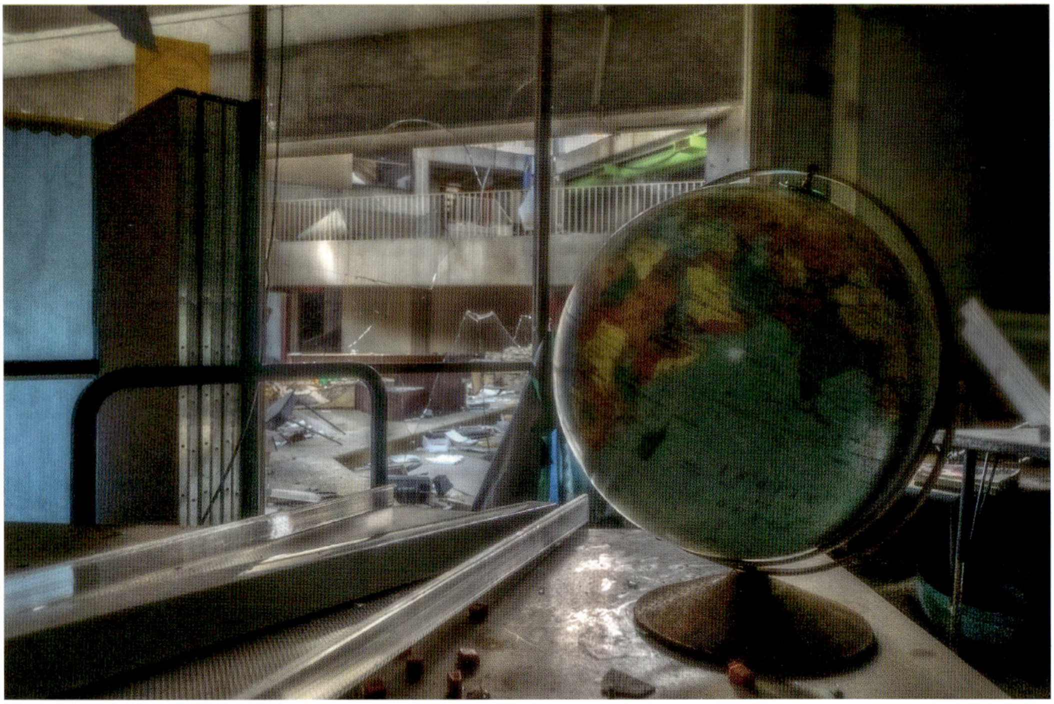

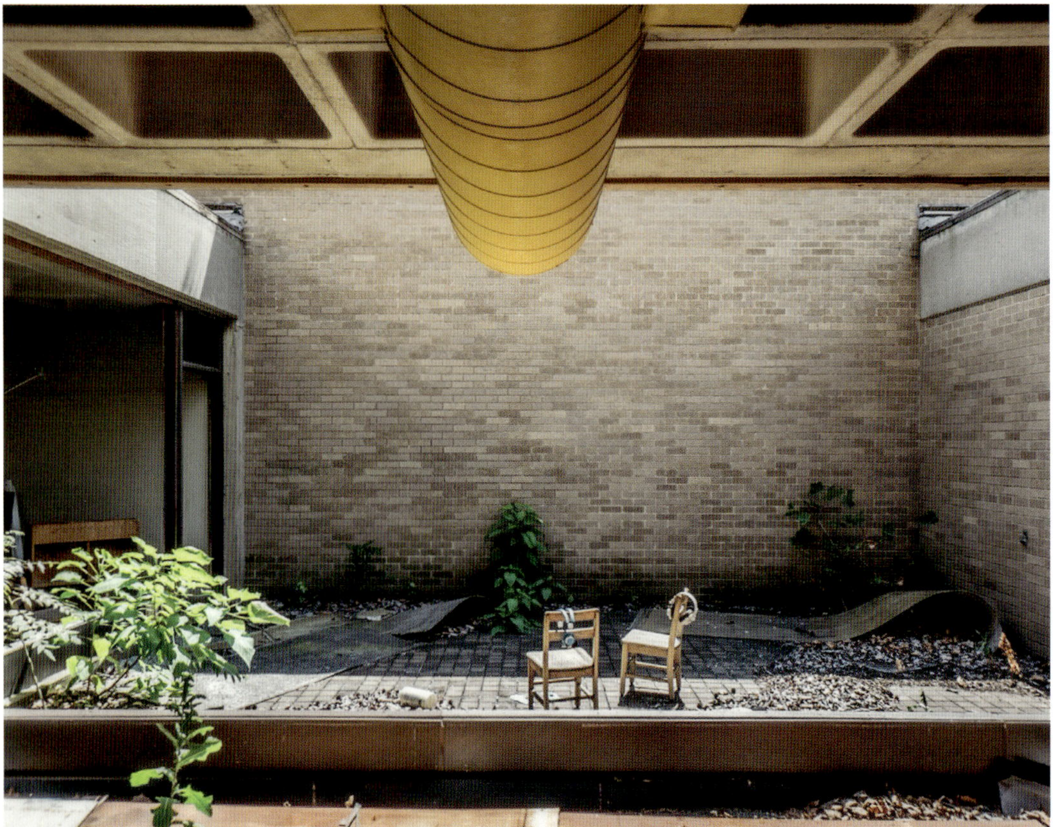

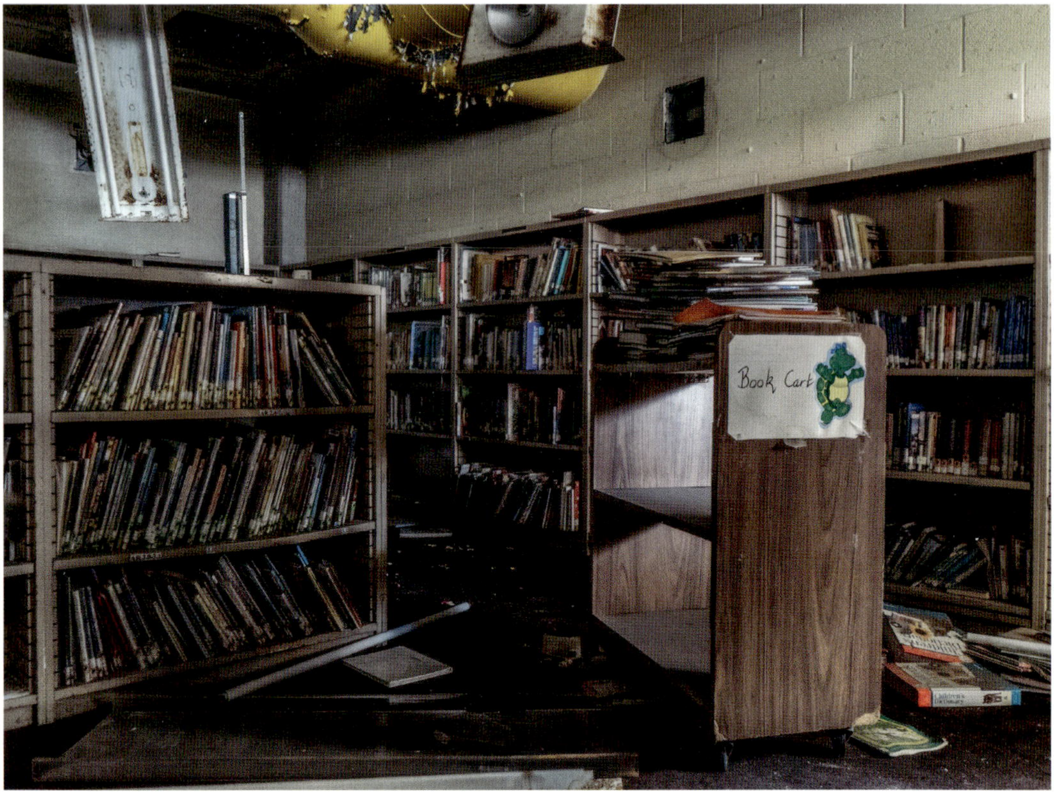
Book Cart

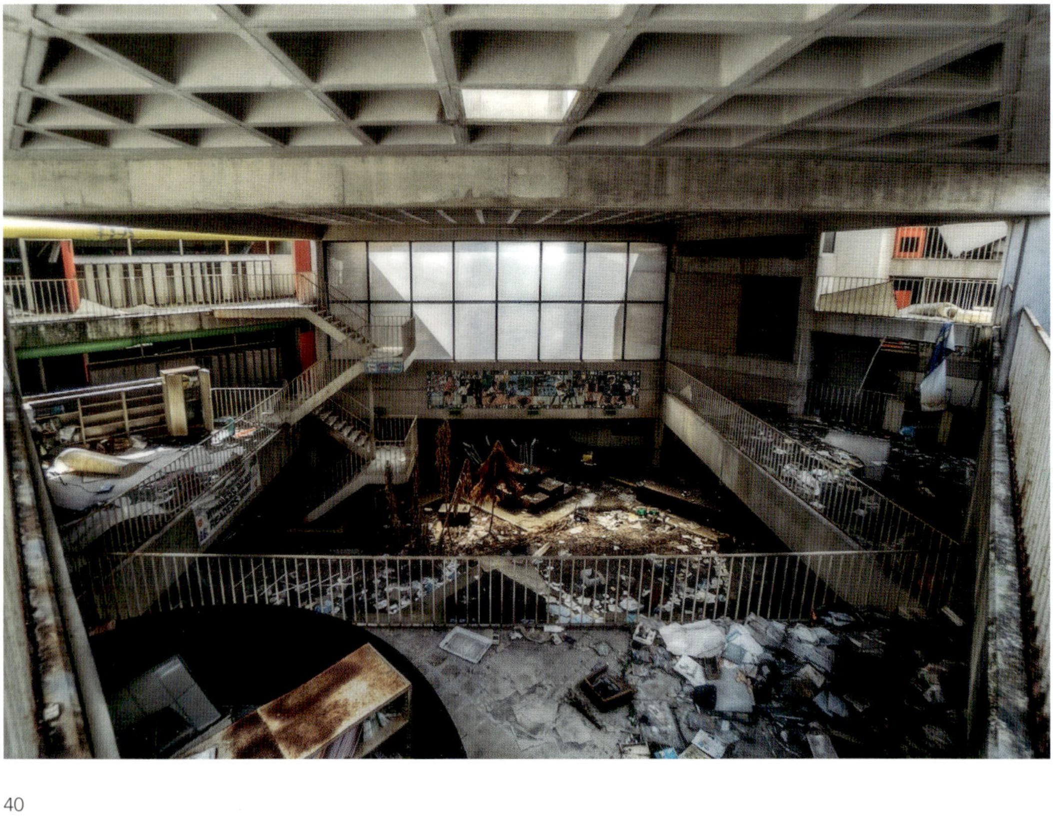

AUDUBON JUNIOR HIGH

Audubon School opened on Cleveland's east side in 1922, teaching grades 6-8. An impressive, three-story gothic-style structure, it featured an auditorium, library, gymnasium, and fifty-four classrooms which could hold more than 1,000 students. A cafeteria and kitchen were added in 1972. One of the school's features, which are remembered fondly by former students, were its "camel humps"—a rear hallway with two sets of stairs running up and down its length, creating the "humps," which were used during physical education class for students to run up and down.

Some of Audubon's notable graduates include Chuck Lampkin and Bob Cunningham, who were the drummer and bassist for famous jazz musician Dizzy Gillespie; as well as Don King, the world-famous boxing promoter who failed both band and gym class while attending the school.

By the millennium, the school had fallen into disrepair, with renovations estimated at more than $2.5 million, and Audubon was another of the sixteen schools closed in 2010. That same year, it was approved for demolition and was listed in Phase II of CMSD's removal plan. The school has since been utilized by the Cleveland Fire Department to run training simulations, but it remains standing as of 2020.

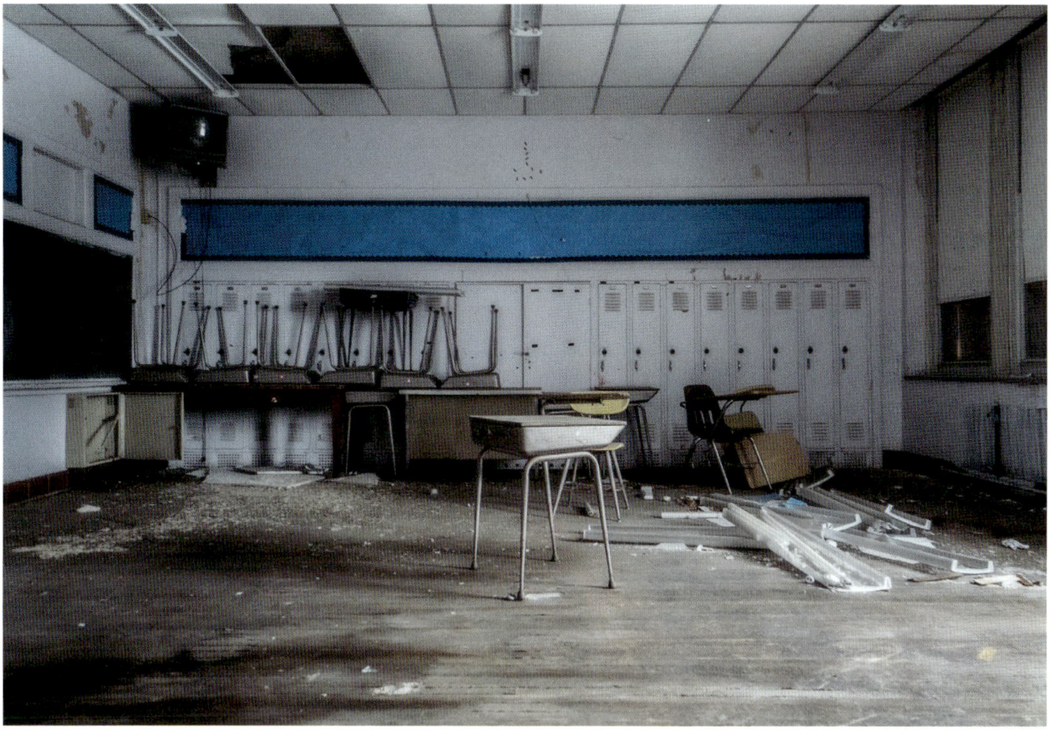

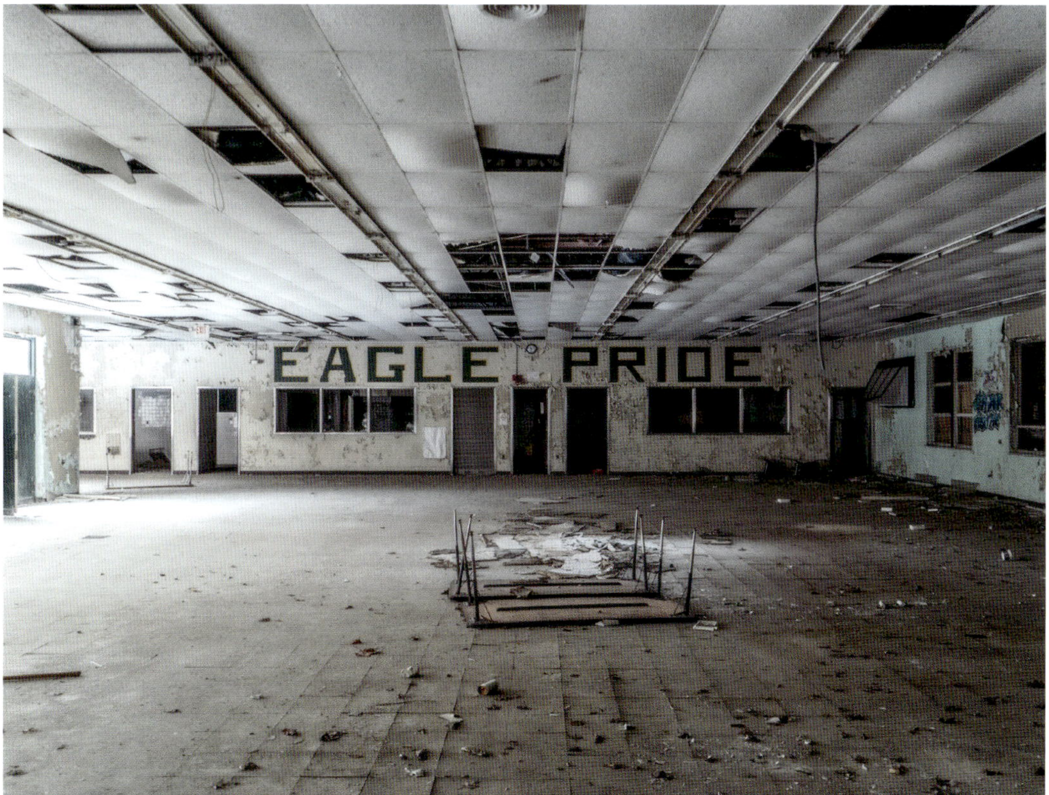
EAGLE PRIDE

—4—
CHURCHES

F ew other places in America have such a diverse array of religion as Cleveland. Christianity was naturally the primary religion of the region's first white settlers, though with the advent of industrialization and many different immigrants flocking to the city, each in turn would found a specific church for their beliefs, leading to more likeminded individuals to move into that neighborhood, as well. The number of different church buildings totaled fifty in 1865, a number which would reach nearly 500 in 1929.

Further churches would spring up not only for the segregated African American population, but also for internal divisions in each religion, some wanting to retain their distinct ethnic roots, while others looked to Americanize. With such a great number of various denominations and religions springing up, each neighborhood still managed to remain primarily centered around one religion, be it the white Protestant west side, Jewish eastern suburbs, or African American east side. These churches were not only the base of the neighborhood religious centers, but also served as the community's social centers, hosting various activities, community services, as well as their own schooling system.

When Cleveland began to fall on hard times, many of the churches were able to remain open, largely in part to the continued donation of faithful remaining members, though many found themselves forced to leave, either from white flight or in search of work. In response, many of the extracurricular activities, as well as the private schools, were closed. But even in the 1990s, one could find more than 1,300 churches, mosques, temples, etc., inside the city. Eventually, that number would begin to dwindle, with the decline in attendance and a lowered donation amount. In 2009, fifty Catholic churches alone were announced as closing or integrating with others.

First Hungarian Reformed

Founded in 1891, this church has the distinction of being the first Hungarian congregation in all of America. The current property was purchased in 1893, and the following year the original wooden church building was finished. Construction on the current building began a decade later, and it was dedicated on Memorial Day 1904.

Referred to as the "stone church" by its congregation, a 1909 city directory notes it as being Calvinistic, a denomination of the Protestant faith. A fire in 1917 destroyed the church interior, estimating damages to almost $200,000 in today's money. The previous year had seen the church purchase a home north on Buckeye

Road to accommodate the growing movement of its congregation to that area, and in 1918, a new brick church was constructed there, permanently closing the former church.

The bells from the original church were removed and have been used in each subsequent building built by First Hungarian, which eventually moved out of the city in 1991. The original building changed hands several times over the following years, finally changing from Second New Hope Baptist to New Community Apostolic in 1989. It is not known when the church was abandoned, but the property landed in foreclosure court in 2017, and was transferred to the Cuyahoga Land Bank. The following year, it was sold to a developer, but remains vacant.

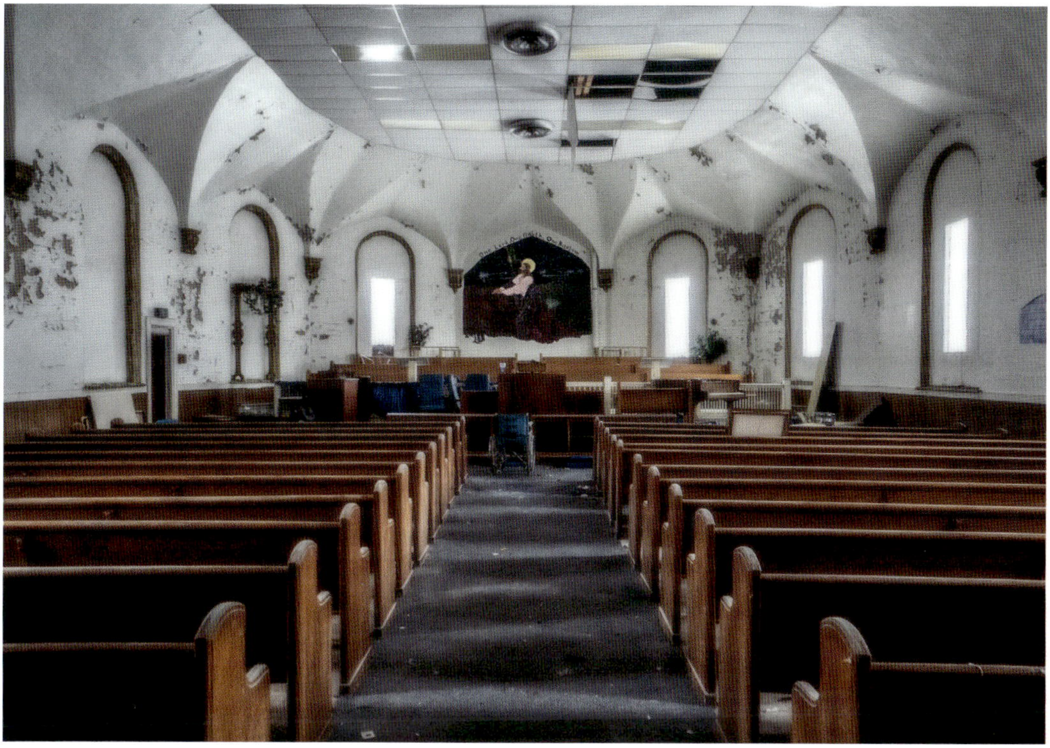

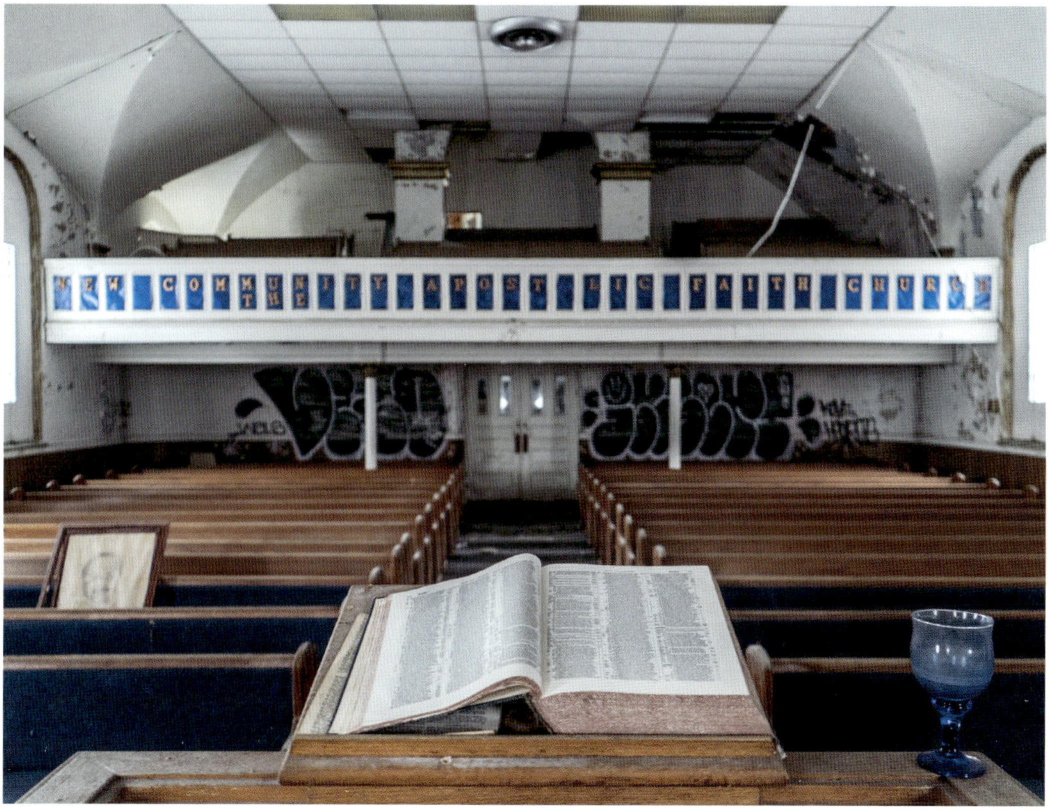
NEW COMMUNITY APOST LIC FAITH CHURCH
THE

NATIVITY OF THE BLESSED VIRGIN MARY

By the early 1900s, the Slovakian community had grown to such an extent in Newburgh that they were able to found their own Slovak Roman Catholic parish. Beginning in rented rooms, The Nativity of the Blessed Virgin Mary (BVM) was founded in 1903, at a cost of $2,500, raised entirely by its congregation, many of whom were only making $1.25 for a twelve-hour workday.

The original church building was constructed on the ground where today's school building sits. In those early years, actual Slovak pastors were in short supply, so pastors of other nationalities were frequently put in charge of the parish, most of whom did not speak their congregation's native language or were unfamiliar with its customs. The following year after its founding, the church rectory was built, and school classes were held on the second story of the church building. In 1909, the congregation received what they were told was another in a string of temporary pastors, Father Chaloupka. Chaloupka, however, would remain serving BVM for over forty-seven years.

With a growing attendance, the school was built in the place of the original church building in 1913. Chaloupka would also purchase property on a nearby island, to be used as a summer camp for the children. By 1924, the congregation had outgrown their church, which could barely hold half of the school's students, let alone their families in one service, and construction began on the current church. At the same time, the school was expanded to a second story, as well as additional wings, and a convent was built later to house the nuns teaching grades 1-8. The school also offered citizenship classes for immigrants and frequently played Slovakian movies, bands, dancing, and featured a bowling alley.

The camp would close in 1944, and the congregation began to dwindle starting in the 1950s. The school closed in 1972, and the Catholic diocese would remove the last permanent priest in 1984. However, BVM remained open until 1992, closing its doors just two days after Christmas. Many religious items, including the altar, pews, and three cast-iron bells were donated to surrounding churches, and the building was sold to Perfected Faith Church, which would close in 2010.

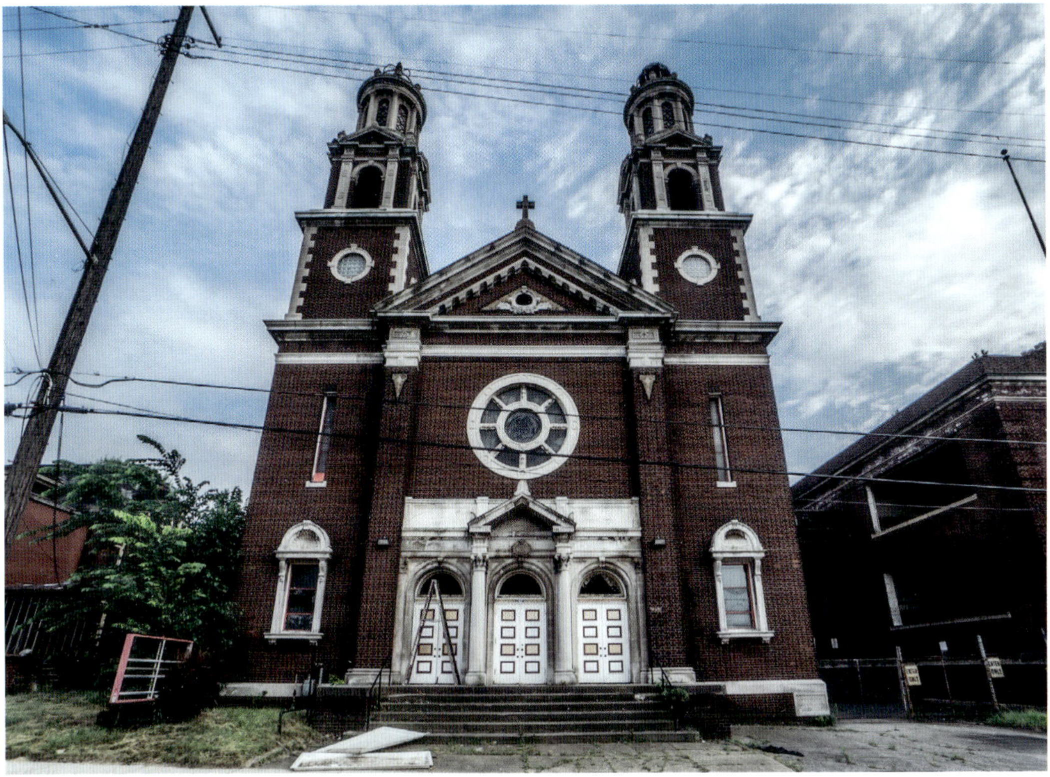

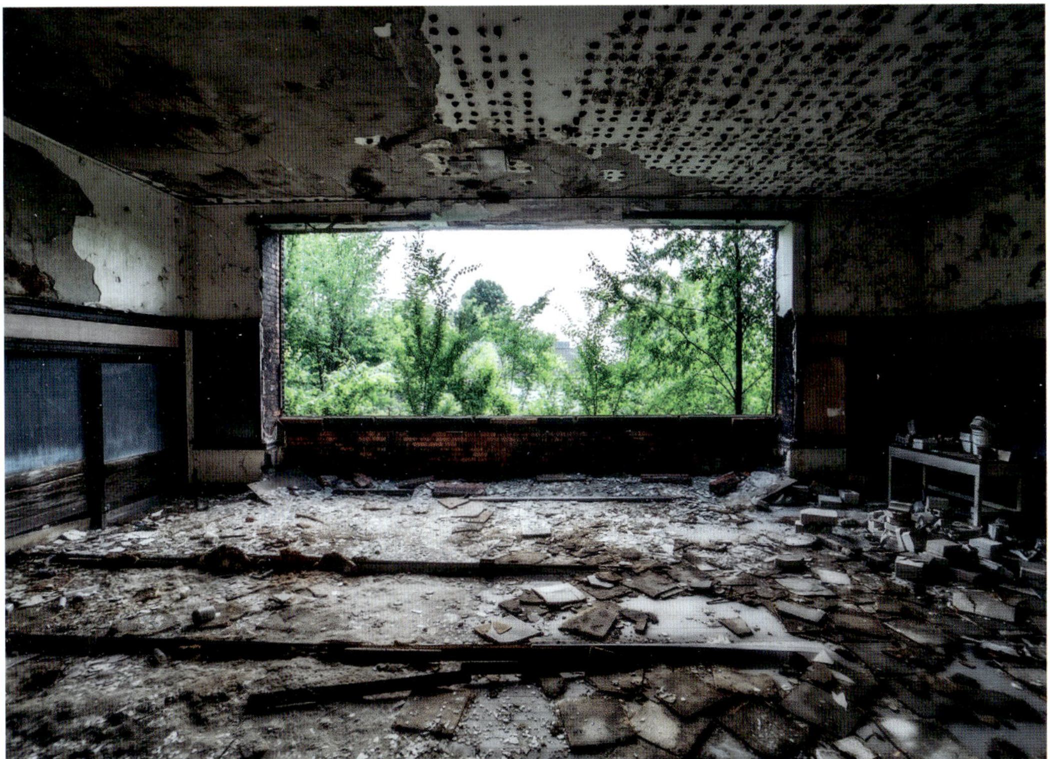

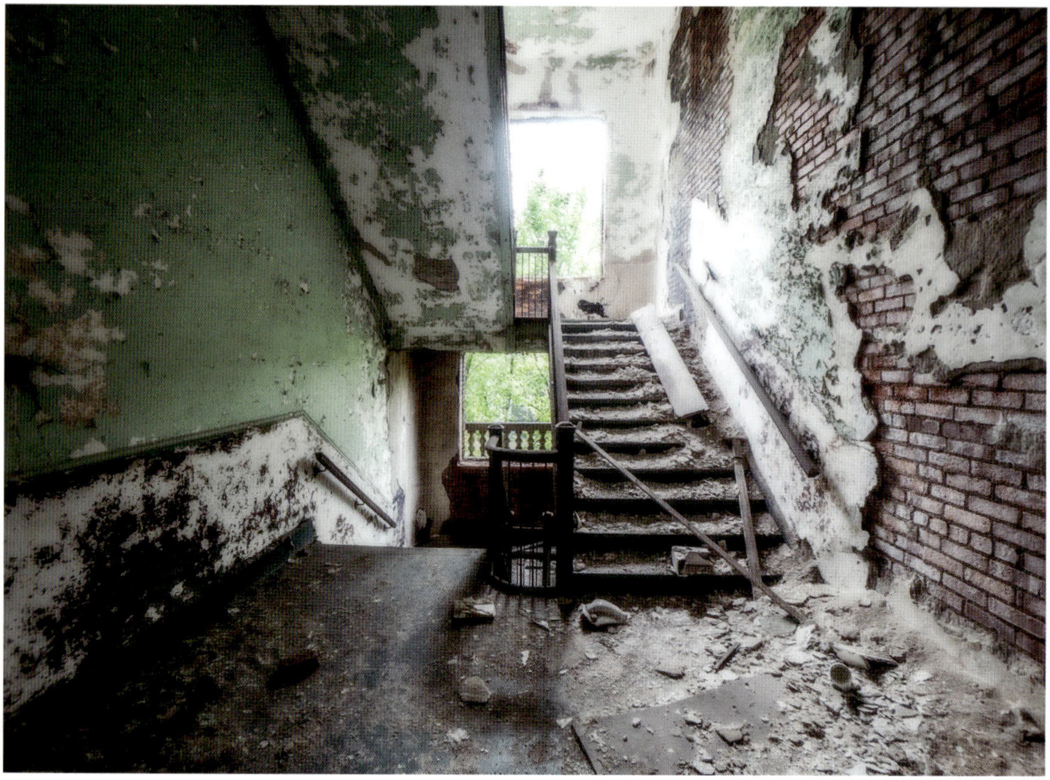

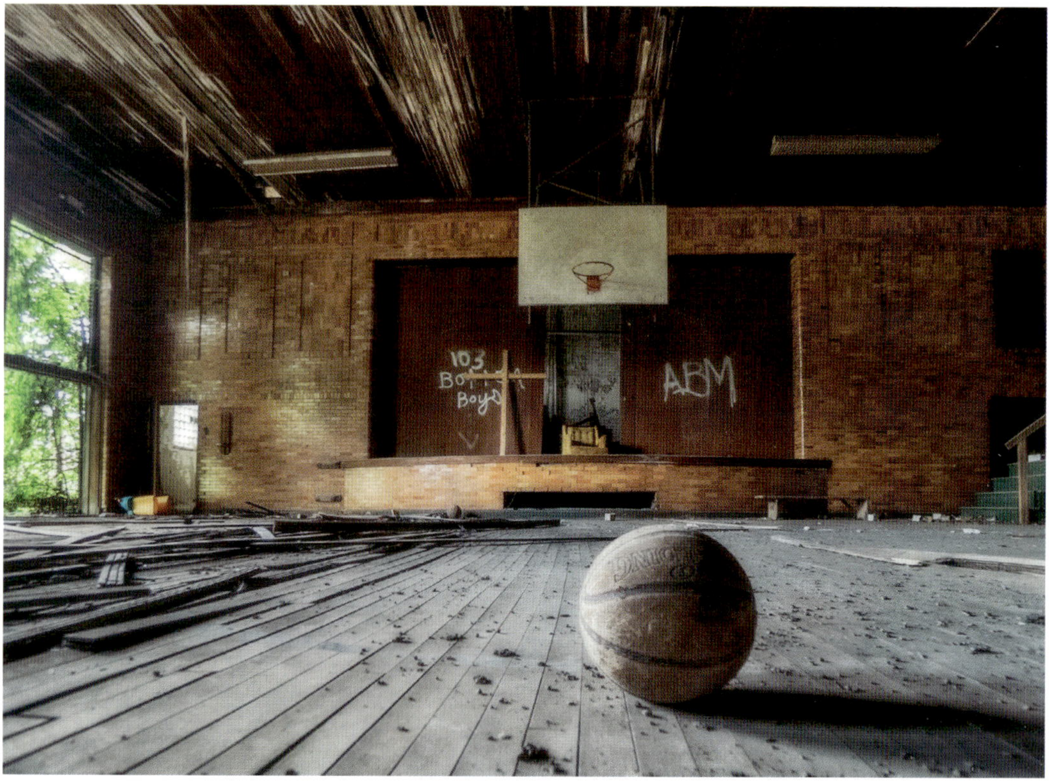
103
ABM

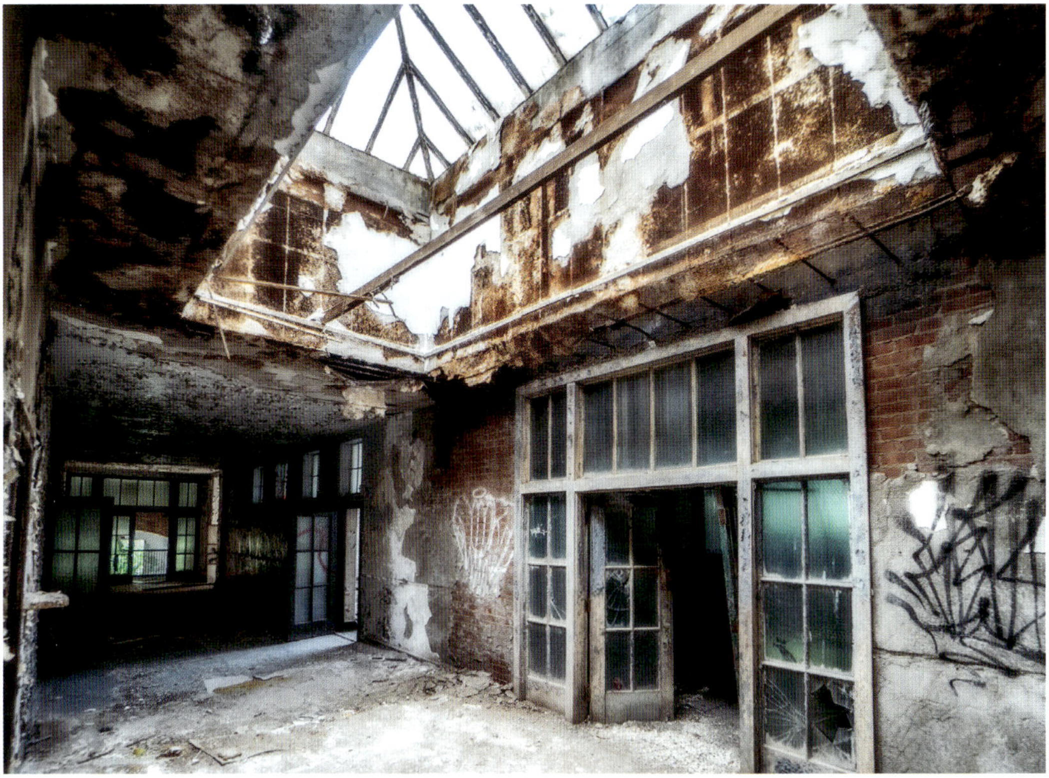

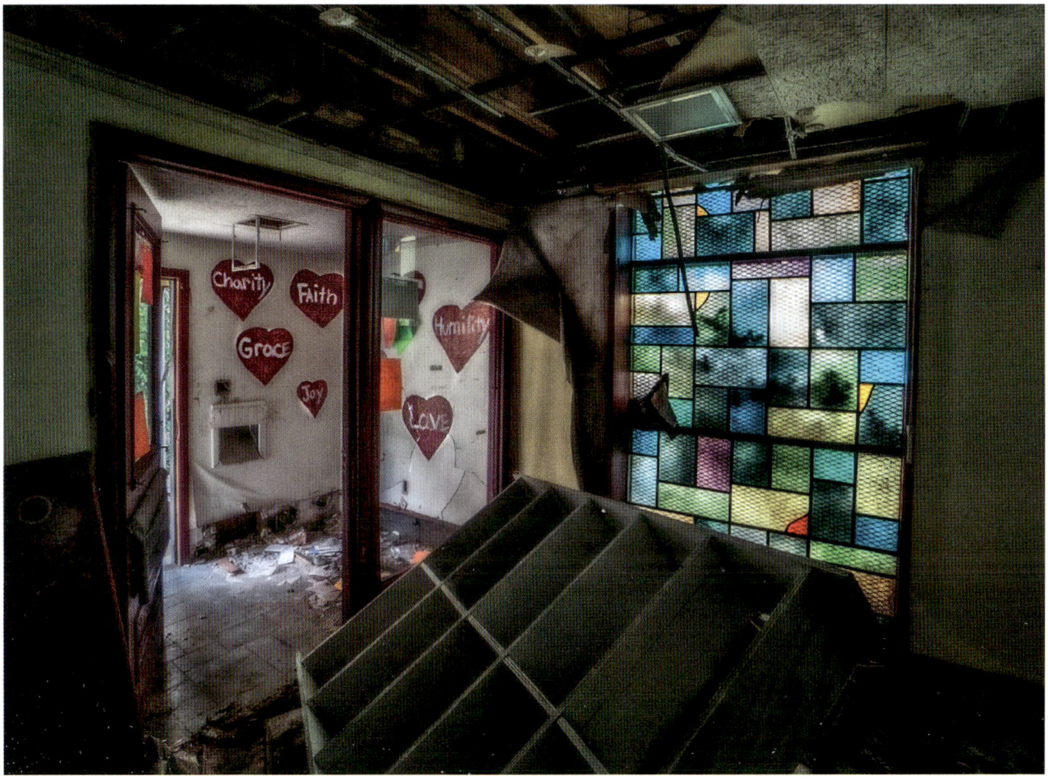
Charity
Faith
Grace
Joy
Humility
Love

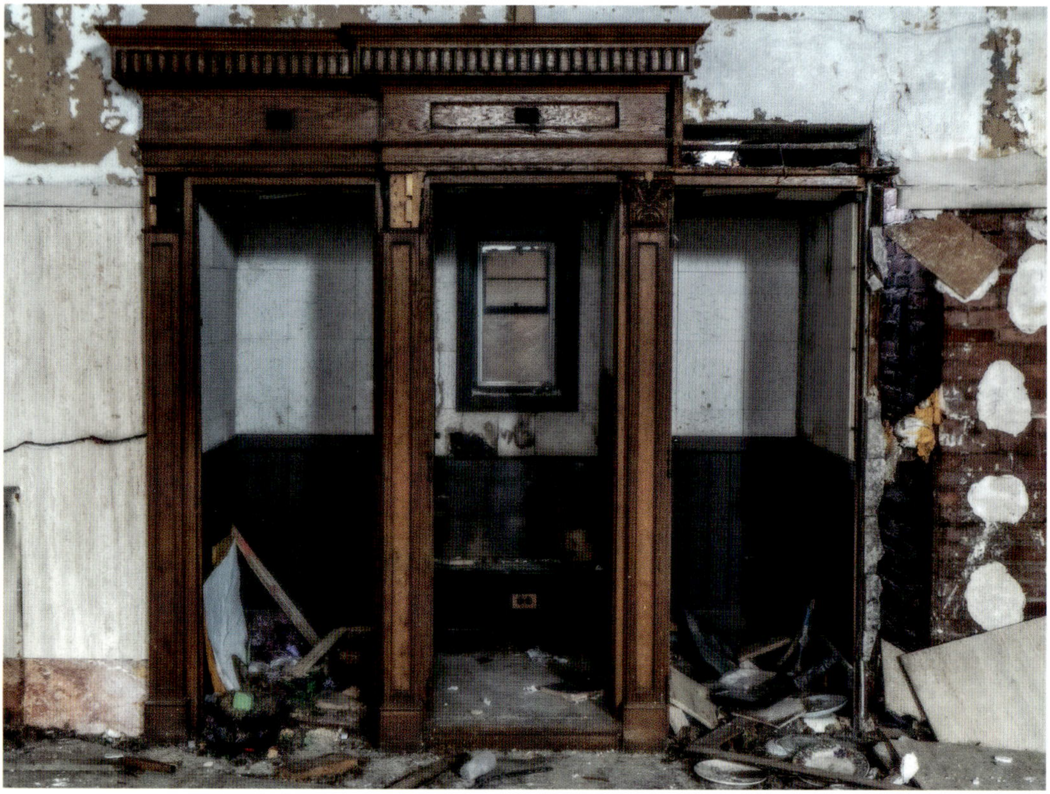

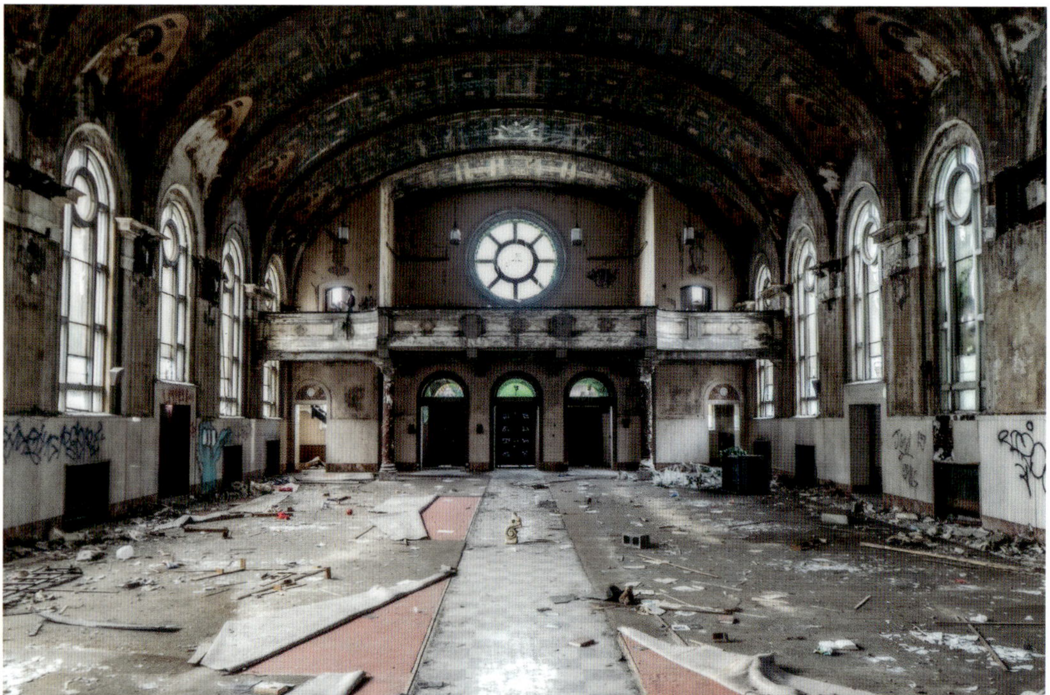

St. Ladislas

St. Ladislas Roman Catholic Church was constructed as a joint effort between Hungarian and Slovakian Catholics, and was the first church for Slovak Catholics in the city. A one-room schoolhouse was built along with the small wooden church in 1889. The partnership was short-lived, however, when on the Sunday service of August 2, 1891, Father John Martvon, one of those hard-to-come-by Slovakian pastors, decided to speak his sermon in Slovak, as opposed to the regular Latin. This set off a riot in the church, with the Hungarians in the congregation shouting "Kill the Slav priest!" The two nationalities began fighting in the pews, while one of the Slovak parishioners guarded Father Martvon with a pistol.

Police eventually arrived before there were any serious injuries and continued to closely monitor the internal struggle for control of the church, which occurred over the next month. Another riot would break out on the lawn of Father Martvon's nearby home before the Magyar Hungarian parish leaders would hire two prominent local attorneys to convince the Cleveland diocese to settle the matter by declaring the church theirs and forcing the Slovaks to build a church elsewhere. Four more meetings would be held, all resulting in shouting matches before the Magyars realized they would not win. Seeing the diocese favoring the church's Slovak pastor, they constructed their own church two blocks down the road, upon a settlement with the Slovaks whereupon they were given $1,000 for the move.

A much grander church was built to the west of the original church, which was then utilized as the school building in 1905, with an additional school building and nun convent being added to the property in the following years. At its height, around 5,000 families attended the church and school, which taught grades 1-8 before closing in 1967, with the building converting to a parish hall. A fire broke out in the basement of the church building on August 8, 1970, leaving the building a ruin, though the next-door hall was left unscathed.

The ruin was demolished the following year and the parish relocated to another city, selling the property. It would eventually end as the somewhat longwinded Festival and Fellowship of Worship in Praise Church of God in Christ in 1997, wisely naming the church a simple Prayer Temple Phase 1. They would remain active, holding events such as revival meetings and women's conferences, until closing in 2014. Today, the convent is gone, the pastor's house is a separate parcel and occupied as a private residence, but the school and original church building which were fought for so desperately over a century before are now abandoned.

—5—
APARTMENT BUILDINGS

E ven in its early days, it was noted that Cleveland had a housing problem, which only grew worse with the city's massive population growth in the early 1900s. Many immigrants moving to the city from their homeland had little money, and a great deal of slums began to form. Apartments would continue to appear in residential areas as a cheaper alternative to those who could not afford houses, which were in short supply as it was. Little was done in the way of public or low-income housing until the mid-1930s, when the city was pushing to clean out the slums.

Apartment complexes would remain in favor as the city's population was shifting to predominantly African American in the 1950s and 1960s. Lowered tourism and increased crime rates saw many hotels closing. Likewise, many high-rises had become ridden with crime, and the police department refused to enter these buildings unless accompanied by one or more fellow officers, even going on strike after they were ordered to do so.

In the more recent years, many apartments have reopened as nursing homes or condominiums. But, for the great deal of buildings too far gone, the government has been tackling demolitions with the same aggression as they do abandoned single-family homes.

COMMUNITY CIRCLE I

This ten-story apartment complex was built in 1973, just west of University Circle and Case Western Reserve. In 1987, it became low-income housing for the elderly along with its nearby sister building, Community Circle II. It featured 160 units, ranging from one or two bedrooms, and advertised a fitness room, rooftop bar, and theater room. The apartments featured stainless-steel appliances, granite countertops, and hardwood floors. Eventually, the property would fall into disrepair. A man was shot and killed in one of the stairwells in 2007, and the apartments would permanently close in 2012.

Perhaps the most interesting story of one of its early tenants comes from a 1979 court case. Two years prior, a nearby bank was robbed by a single black male, who made off with $552 cash. Witnesses saw the fleeing man enter a car, with its license plate subsequently traced to a resident of the apartment building. Upon being questioned, it was determined that the tenant across the hall had used the car. FBI agents questioned the apartment's owner, who invited them in where his roommate, John Henry Reeves, was cooking dinner. The agents noticed a pair of jeans and a blue denim jacket in Reeves' room, the same outfit worn by the robber. Reeves was subsequently arrested and convicted.

Above left: Apartment 10G, where Reeves lived.

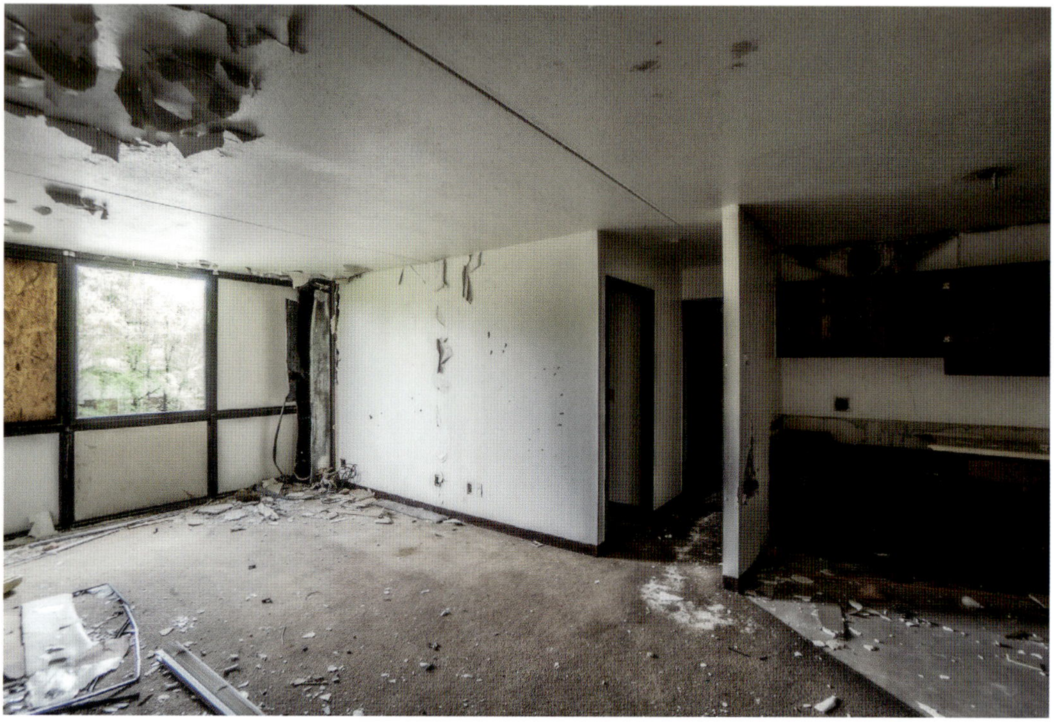

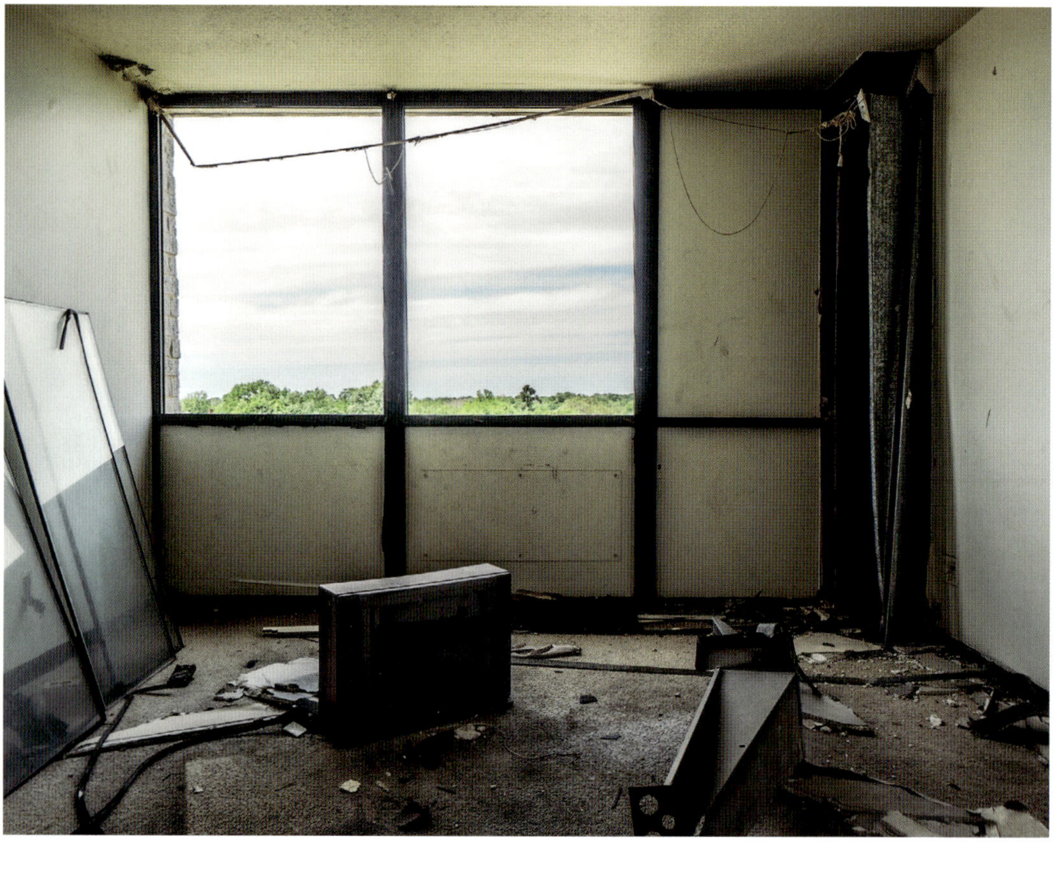

THE STRAWBERRY MURDERS

In 1989, the bodies of several women were found strangled and dumped in abandoned apartment buildings off Hayden and First avenues. It would be over twenty years until one of those murders was solved, though there are some clear suspects in the other two cases.

Much of the area between Hayden and 133rd Street consists of apartment complexes, mostly built in 1925. The King's Court apartment complex was later constructed in 1958, likely replacing homes or some of the original buildings. Like Elderwood, many of these apartments would become abandoned when the area's crime rate rose in the 1980s.

In 1986, the first victim was found in the courtyard of an abandoned apartment complex; she was strangled with a red ribbon, but also had been beaten with a lead pipe so severely that it was reported, "Her face is gone." Two years later, a woman was found strangled inside her home on Hayden Avenue. The following winter, a pregnant woman was found frozen inside an abandoned apartment building on First Avenue. The next month, the body of yet another woman was found inside another abandoned apartment building on that same street, a red ribbon left wrapped around her neck, as well.

The cases were nicknamed the "Strawberry Murders" in the media; "strawberry" being a slang word for sex workers, as at least two of the women had previous arrests for prostitution. The cases were never solved, and eventually shelved due to the overwhelming amount of new crimes, budget problems, and lack of manpower in the police department.

That all changed in 2009 with the arrest of Cleveland serial killer Anthony Sowell. As mentioned previously, Sowell moved to the area in 1985 and his primary method of killing was strangulation. He even knew the third victim, who lived on the same street as him, but nothing was ever conclusively linked to him. However, authorities did get a DNA hit to another convicted killer, Joseph Harwell.

Already serving a life sentence for a 1997 murder, Harwell had previously served six years for attempting to strangle a woman in 1989. The DNA evidence would conclusively link Harwell with the first victim, as well as another woman murdered in 1996, but without a confession and no DNA evidence in the other two murder cases, they remain unsolved to this day.

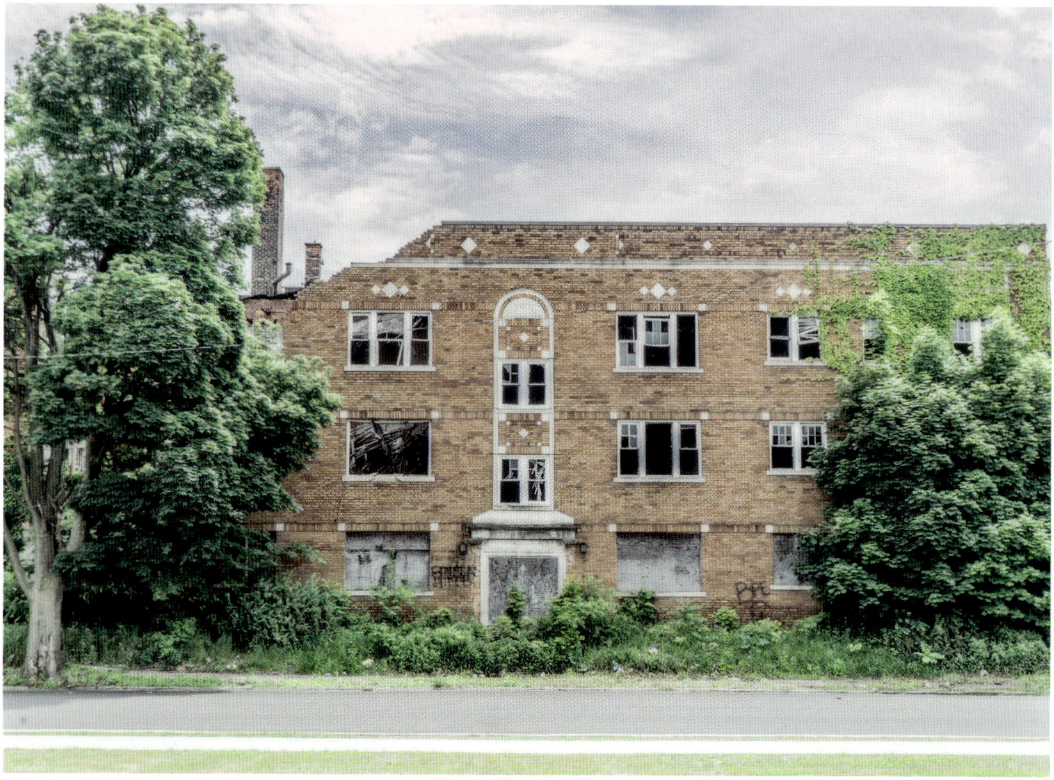

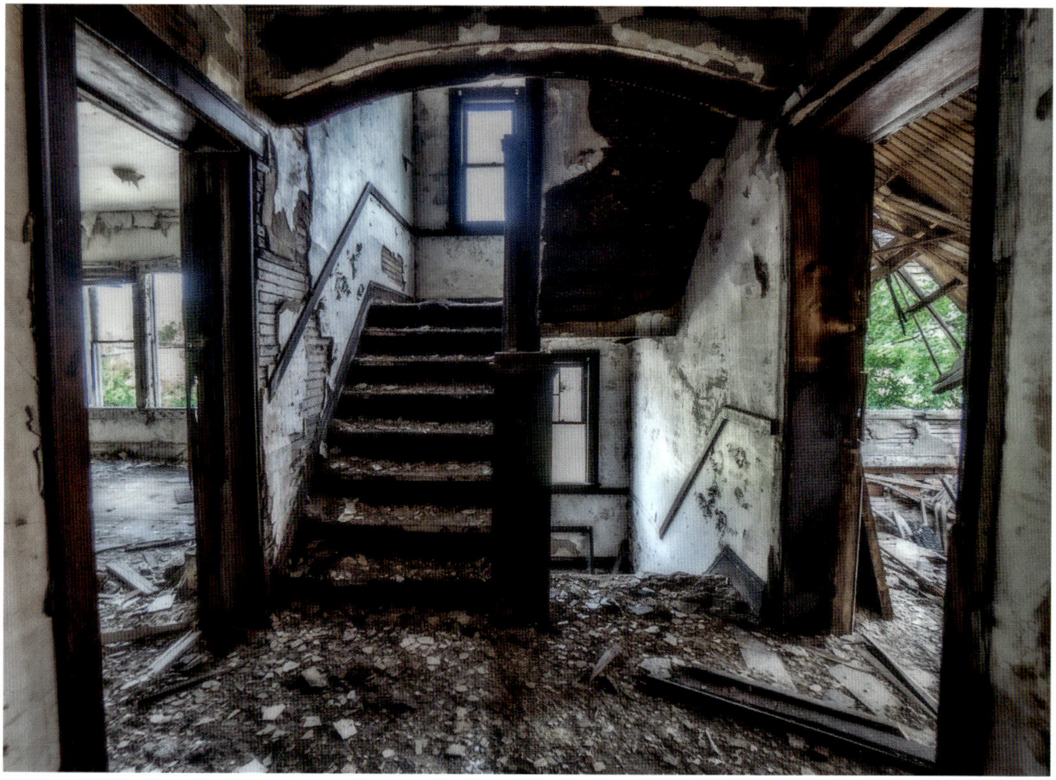

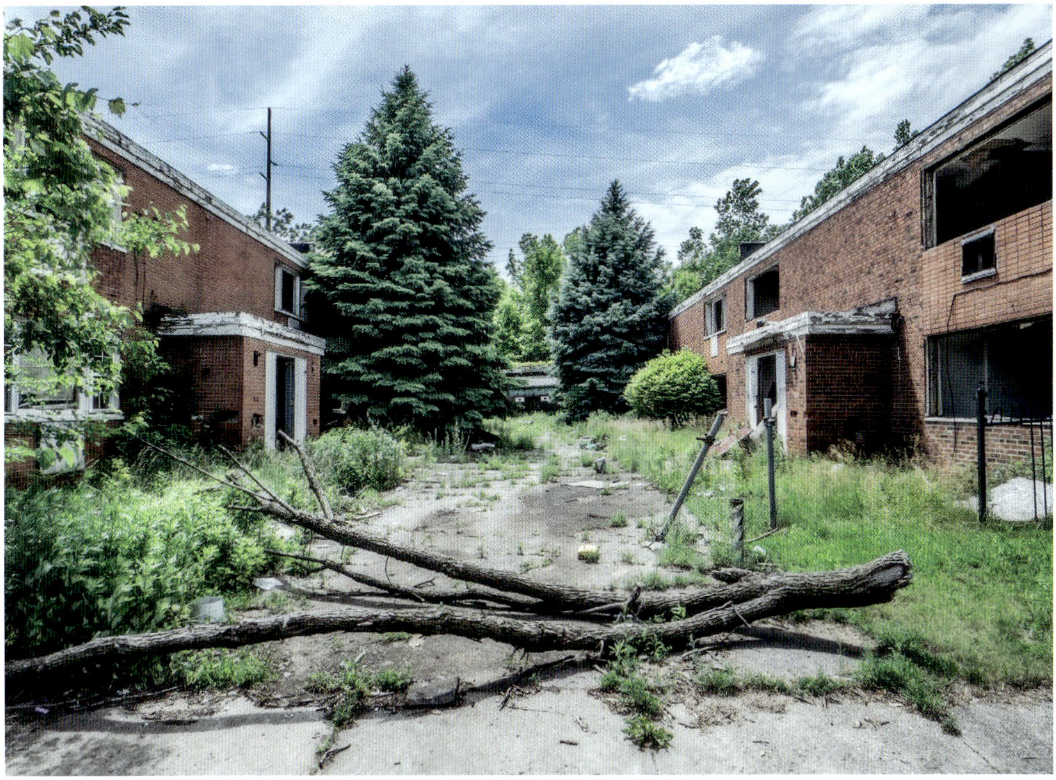

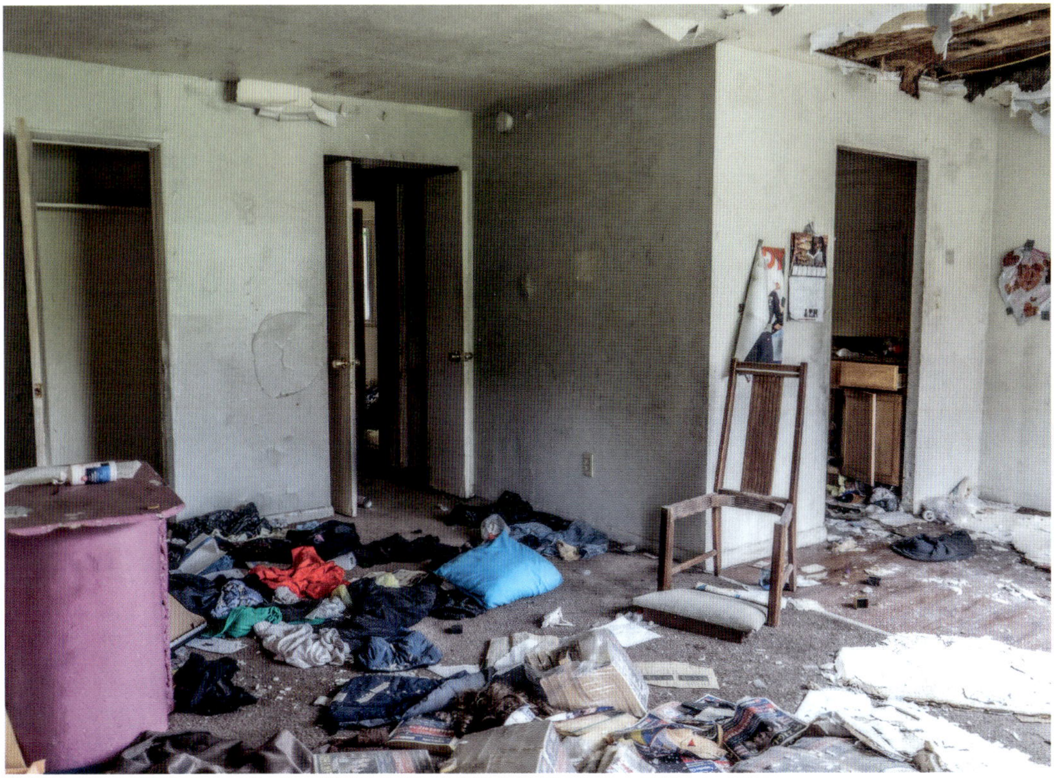

Sarah Redman Apartments

This four-unit apartment complex overlooking Rockefeller Park was built in 1910. It has housed numerous well-to-do socialites over the years, including the president of the Anderson Millinery, an apparel company that has since faded into obscurity.

The building entered probate court in 1979 and was given to two women, presumably the deceased owner's daughters. The following year, it was foreclosed on and sold to the Lutheran Housing Corporation, which provided affordable housing to local residents. It was sold in 1984 and was then transferred between family members multiple times over the years until the Department of Housing took ownership in 2008.

The property was next transferred to the landbank until finally ending in the hands of a community development organization. Being historically designated in 2013, the apartments are planned to become the Cleveland Cultural Gardens Welcome Center. A request for $170,000 in state aid was made in 2019; however, the building did not win one of the five grants that year.

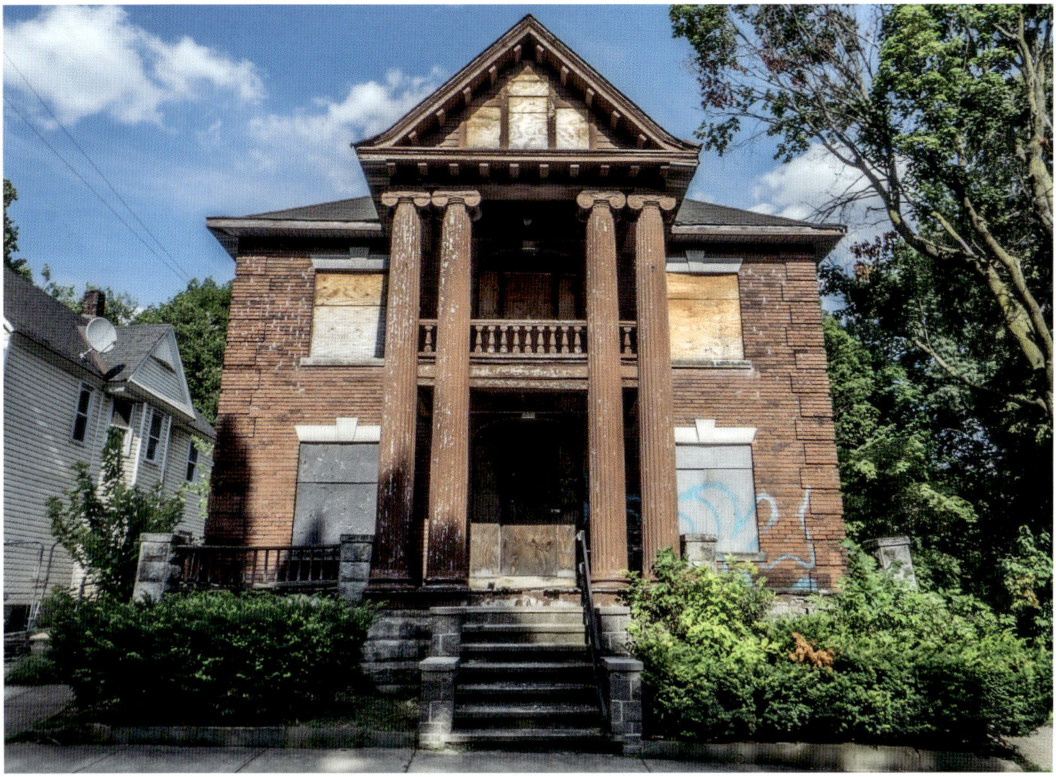

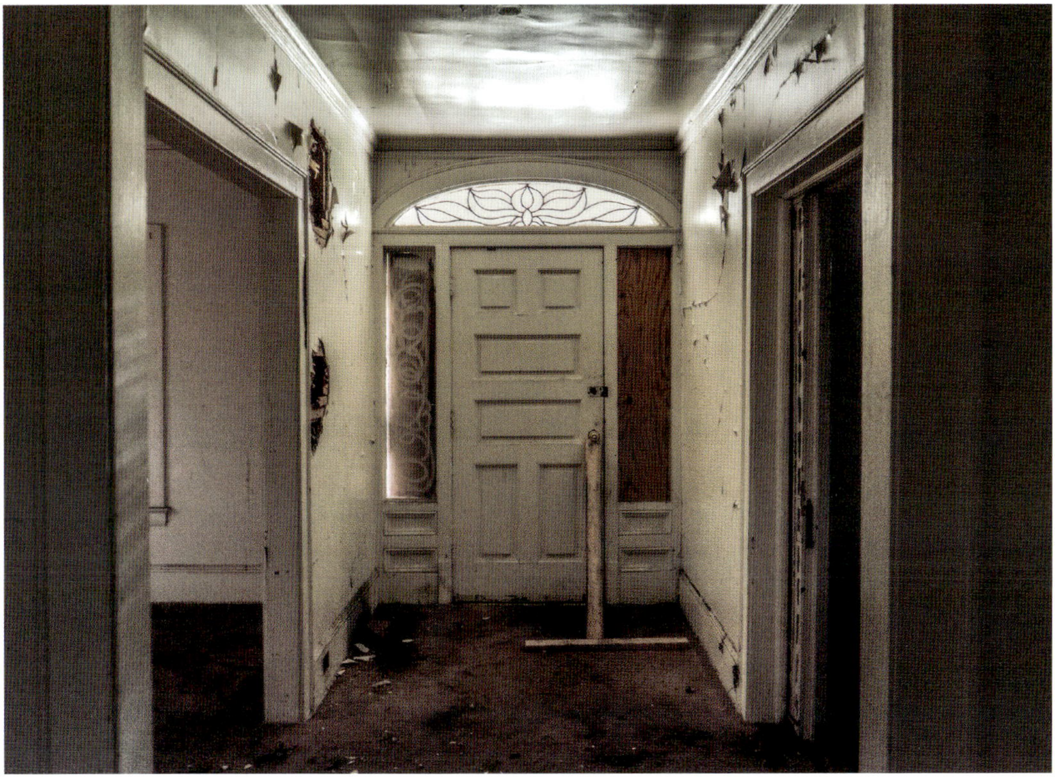

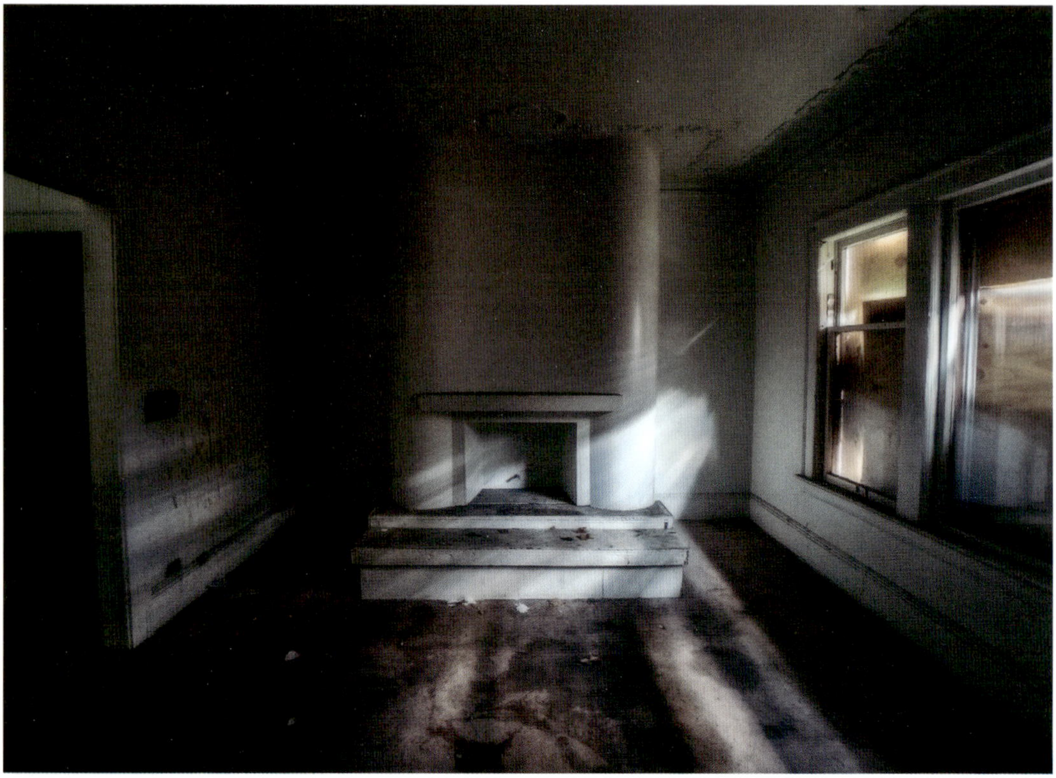

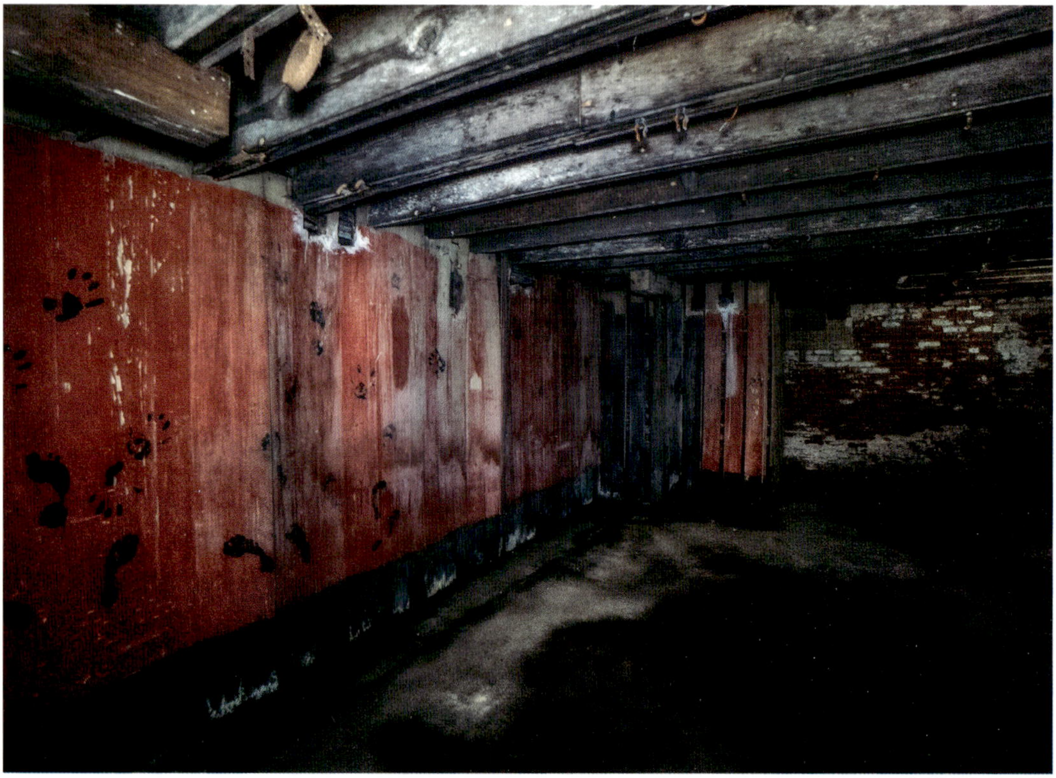

—6—
HEALTH AND GOVERNMENT

With the advent of becoming a city, Cleveland would expand its government and services, establishing the Superior Court of Cleveland in 1847. Two years later, it would start a hospital and poorhouse, where financially burdened citizens could stay. The following few decades would see the beginnings of numerous other services, including the waterworks, fire department, and public library, as well as the unique needs of the numerous immigrant groups living in the city.

These new services saw increased expenditures as the city grew, leading to the city frequently needing to borrow additional money. The early 1900s saw more services such as garbage, street cleaning, tuberculosis hospitals, and juvenile court being established.

The city's debt would nearly double by 1906, and the government would quickly find that many of the blooming suburbs around the city were growing independent from Cleveland, which had decidedly inferior city services than what the suburbs could provide for themselves. The Great Depression would put further strain on the city, which was tasked with creating public housing and social welfare benefits.

By the time industries began to vacate, the city was faced with a number of problems including riots in the African American ghettos, lowered tax income, and an unwillingness to cooperate from the remaining businesses and banks, which had been targeted in 1977 by the newly elected mayor who fought against the privileges they were enjoying. In response, the banks refused to roll over some of the city's debts, leading to the city of Cleveland defaulting on its loans.

A new mayor was elected in 1979, who set about repairing the damaged relations with the banks and businesses, but other problems remained. More than half of the city's budget in 1986 was spent on the Department of Public Safety, which had to contend with the drug epidemic, rampant gang violence, fires, and more. As residents fled, the lost revenue from those now-absent taxpayers forced the city to make numerous cuts to its services. The police department was forced to cut 251 officers in 2004 alone, and firefighters were forced to contend with rodent problems in their stations.

HOUSE OF WILLS

Originally opening in 1904, the House of Wills moved to its final building in 1941. Until its closure, it was the oldest and most successful black-owned business in the city. The property was abandoned for some time until being purchased. While it is still not actively used, the owner occasionally allows ghost hunters and photographers inside. However, a lesser-known second location was opened in 1987 on Harvard Avenue.

Both locations were owned and operated by the Wills family until closing in 2013, when serious problems surfaced. Prior to closing, the owner offered prepaid funeral services to families; however, when those families went to use their policies, they were informed by the insurance company that those policies had already been collected by the owner of the now-closed business.

In all, at least sixteen families were robbed of the policies that they had been paying into for years. The former owner pleaded guilty to insurance fraud, forgery, and grand theft to one of the sixteen—the others were never brought to court. She was sentenced to repay the family, as well as community service.

The following year, it was discovered that sensitive personal records required to be properly secured or destroyed remained inside the wide-open, abandoned funeral home. The files were removed, and the property was eventually sold in a sheriff's auction in 2018. It was demolished that November.

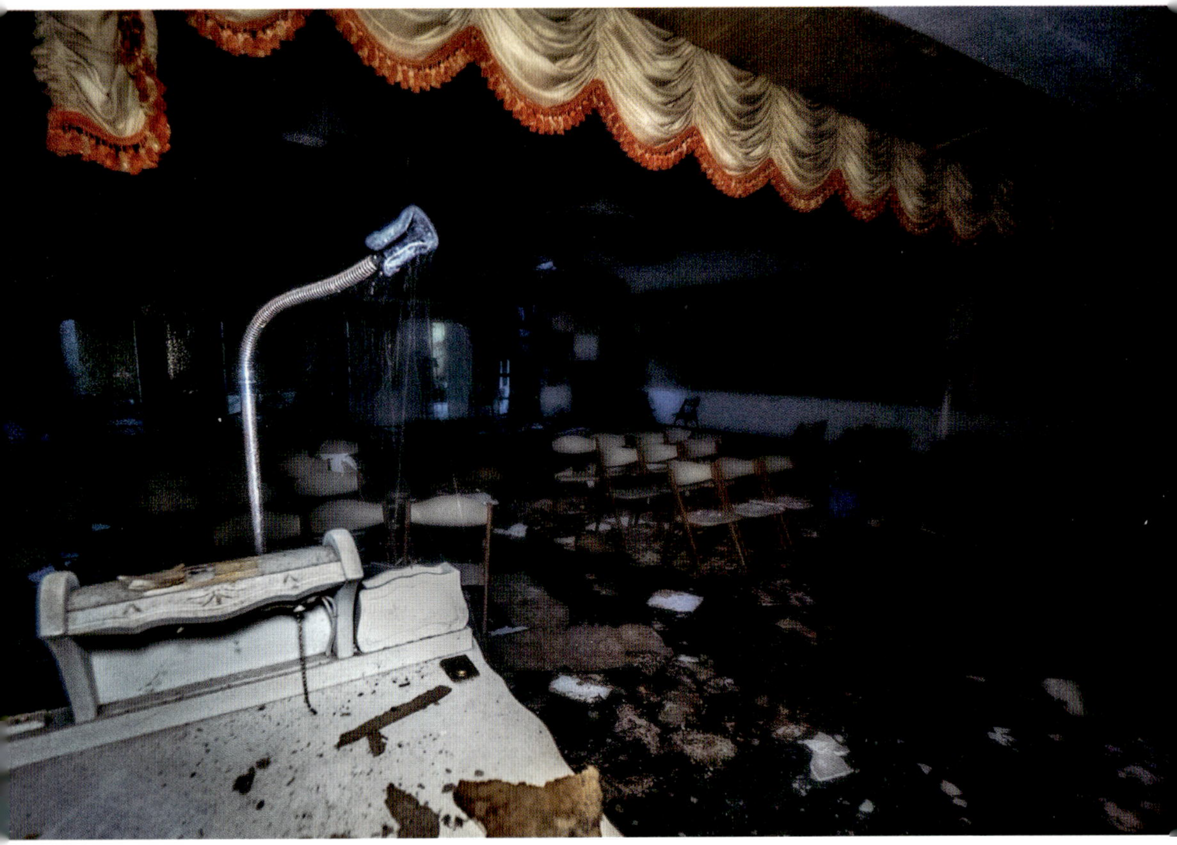

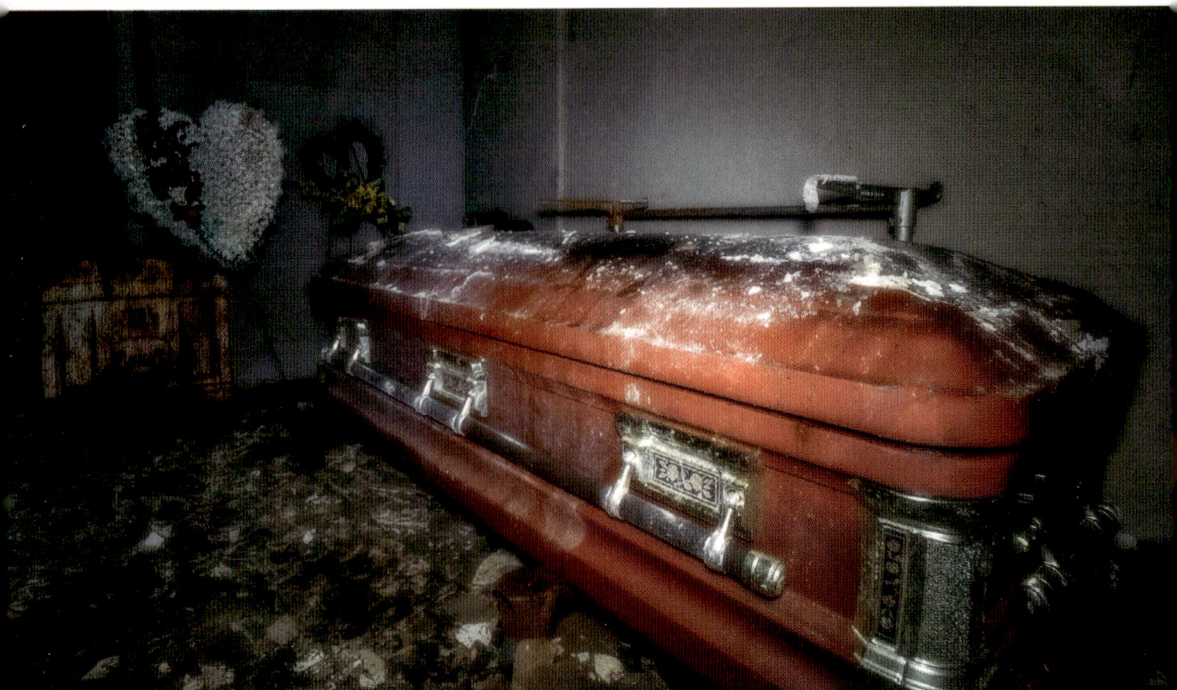

SUPERIOR LIBRARY

In 1903, business tycoon Andrew Carnegie donated $250,000 to the Cleveland Public Library to expand their branches. This resulted in the construction of four-teen new libraries across the city between then and 1920, the final building being the Superior Branch. This building and many of the other Carnegie libraries were designed by Andrew's brother-in-law and architect, Henry Whitfield.

Previously, Superior was a much smaller sub-branch and reports complain of the building being quite congested. A book drive was held in 1918, which notes Superior as collecting roughly 15,000 books inside a full-size sleeping tent that was set up as a window display and receptacle for the donated books, though judging by the reports from other branch collections, that may be a typo meant to be 1,500 books.

Construction on the new building began in September 1919, and was due to be completed January 1, 1920; however, a plasterer strike delayed the opening until September. In the meantime, it is mentioned that the library's temporary location was even more crowded than its previous location, with all departments condensed to a small double-door storeroom. The children's department was located between a section of shelves, and only took up roughly eight square feet. The rest of the library's books were stored in boxes in front of the shelves, which had to be moved as needed.

Finally, the new location opened with a total of eighteen employees. Furniture for the library arrived slowly, with the large reading tables not coming until December. Because of this, the grand "Opening Day" was, in fact, not celebrated for six months after the library actually opened. More than 400 people came; however, the planned musicians did not show up for the event, and the orchestra from a local church filled in at the last minute. Almost 10,000 people were registered at Superior to borrow books. The building also featured a section of club rooms, which were utilized by 135 different groups for meeting space.

By the 1970s, the neighborhood would change like much of Cleveland, and Superior saw many surrounding businesses and homes becoming vacant. The library also found new challenges, as many visitors were illiterate or poor readers, who preferred the library's audio/visual department, while the books were left largely to gather dust. Book circulation dropped from almost 24,000 checked out in 1960, to less than 4,000 in 1975. To survive, the library canceled numerous magazine subscriptions and cut its book collection down to 10,700, completely closing the upstairs rooms, which were rented out to a renovation and restoration company.

In a community of roughly 20,000, Superior reportedly had only about fifty regular patrons, with about 200 others showing up once or twice a year, before it was closed for good in 1990. Two years later, the building opened as The Children's Comprehensive Learning Center, which closed in 1999.

BALDWIN MANOR NURSING HOME

This thirty-one-unit complex was built in 1968 as a second nursing facility to Mapleside Nursing, which was already utilizing the former mansion of architect Levi Scofield up the hill they had purchased in 1955. The mansion was built in 1902 by Scofield, who had worked on the Schofield [sic] hotel, as well as the Ohio State Reformatory in Mansfield.

This new building cut into the hill the mansion was perched on, removing its driveway and thereby only allowing access from the back of the property. Mapleside was renamed Baldwin Manor in 1987 and the mansion facility was closed shortly after. Originally ninety-eight beds, the newer facility was converted to just forty-one beds, though at the time of its closure it was running at half capacity. The owners cited that the facility could not compete against newer nursing homes with more amenities. Residents reported that they were given just forty-eight hours to vacate in 2006, a timeframe which was extended to the proper ninety days when the story was picked up by the news.

The following year, the building became the Youth Devoted to Christ Ministry, until the landbank assumed ownership in 2012 when it entered tax foreclosure. The property then was purchased by a woman planning to convert the nursing home into a treatment center for recovering drug addicts. At the time of purchase, she was unaware the property included the mansion. The county took control again in 2016 when the buildings were condemned, as the owner was unable to gain funding and had not paid any taxes on the property.

The Scofield mansion was saved from demolition when it was declared a historic site and the building was cleaned and secured. The same designation was not given to the nursing center.

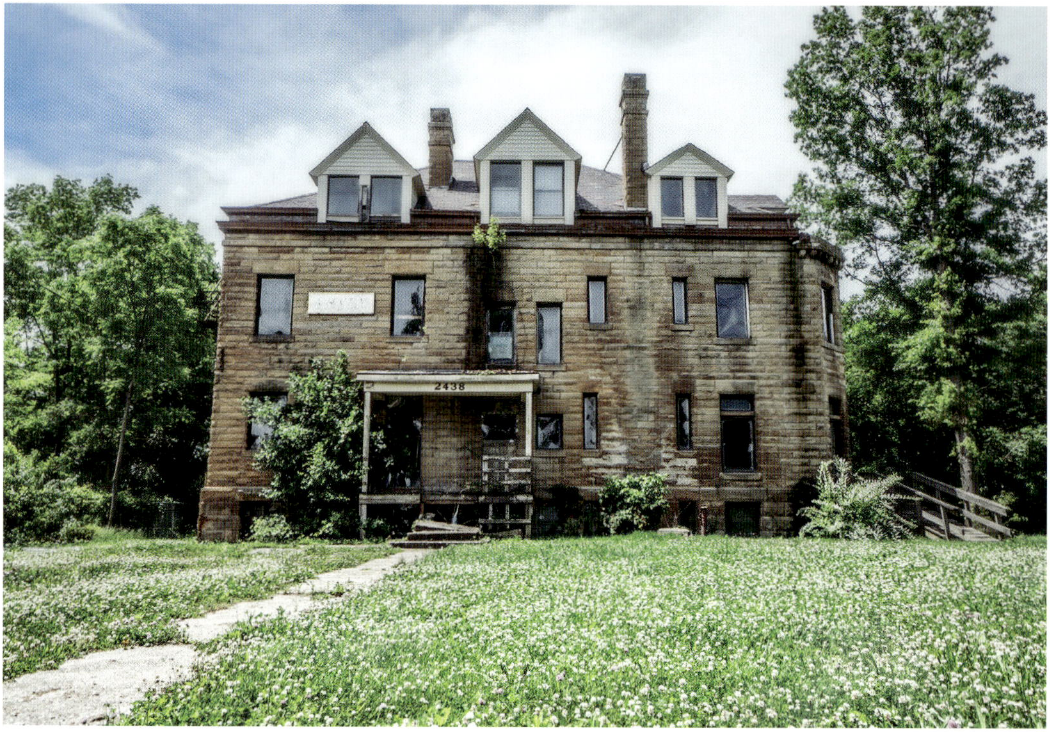
2438

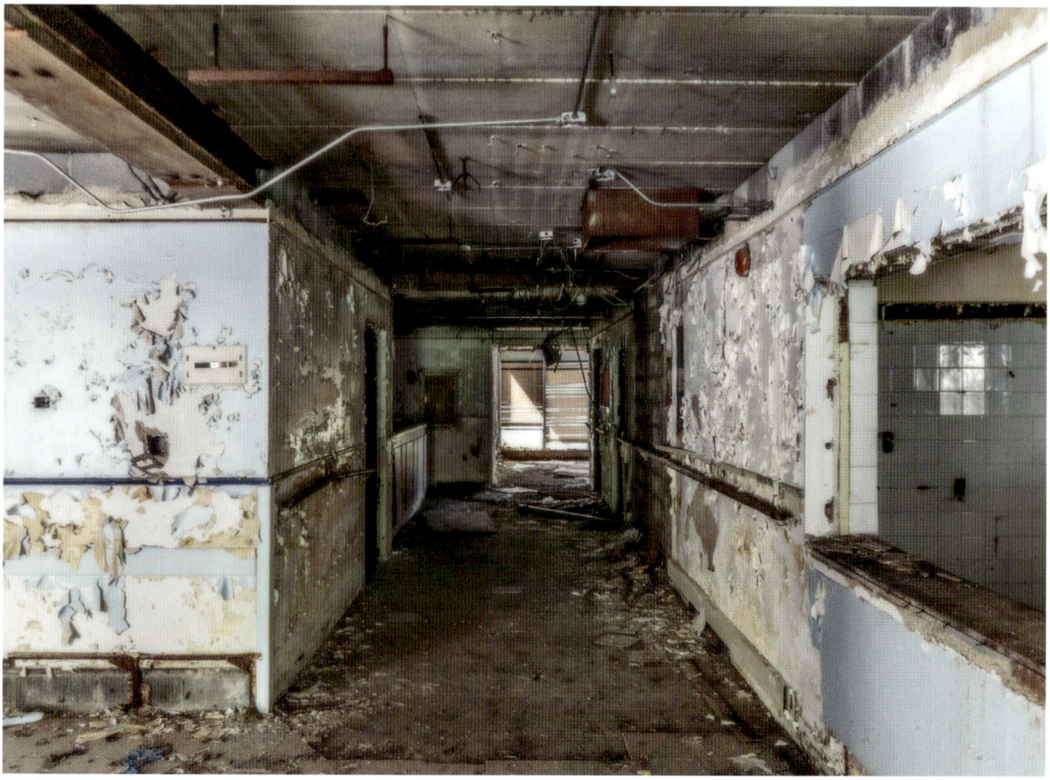

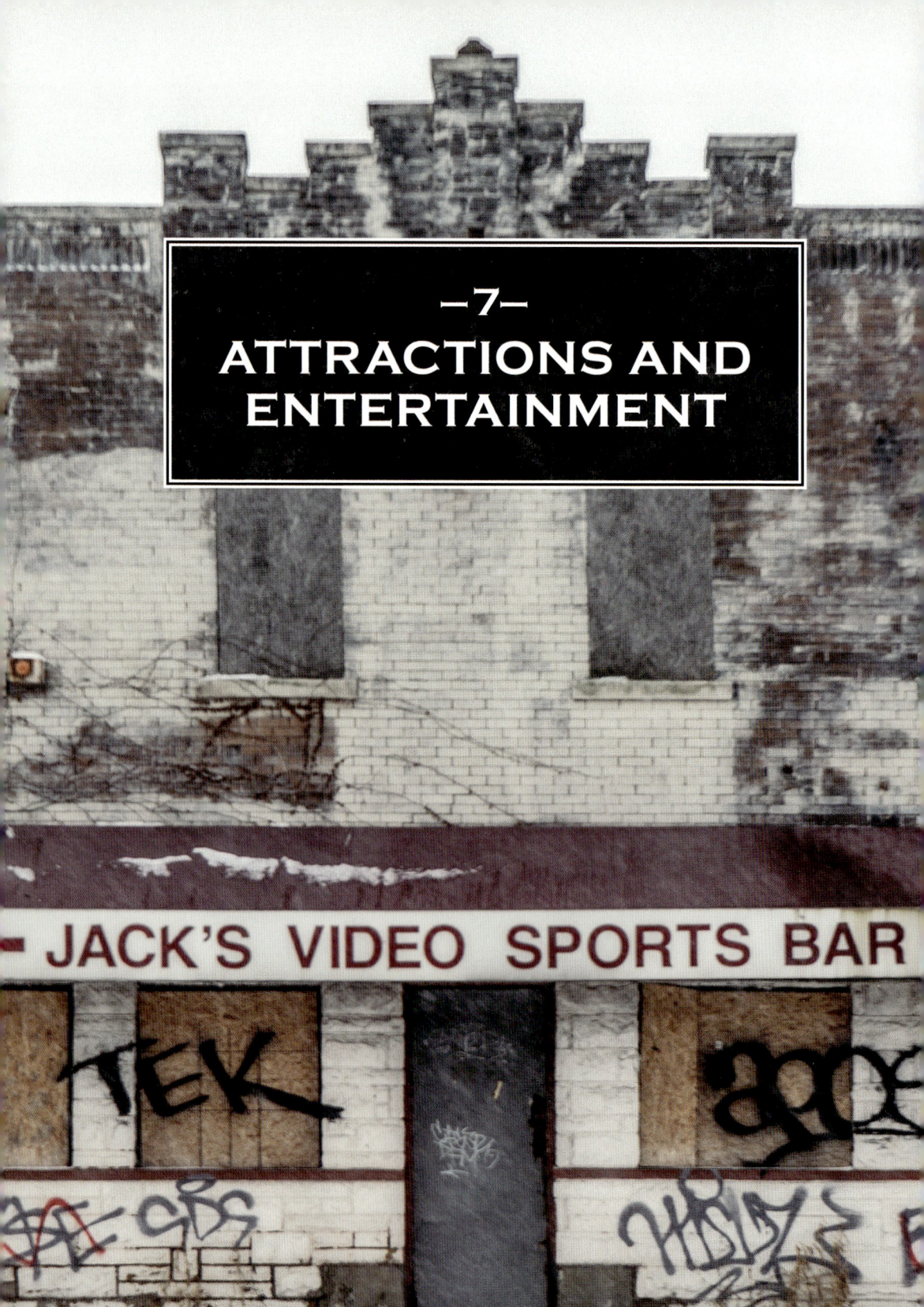

–7–
ATTRACTIONS AND
ENTERTAINMENT

F inding itself losing much of its industry, the city needed a new approach to draw in revenue. Beginning in the 1990s, Cleveland began to market itself as a destination city, a place with museums, sports, zoos, and more that would attract visitors who in turn would spend their money in the city so desperate for the revenue. But Cleveland has had a long history of attractions and entertainment prior to this, as the need for entertainment arose in its early years.

In its growth period, housing was the primary need for neighborhoods. Thusly, the population found themselves living in a cramped area with little to do outside of their ethnic events held at their churches. Lured by this large, centralized population, many who had extra money to spend from their high-paying factory jobs, places such as Forest City Theme Park, opened in 1893 to more than 100,000 visitors its first year.

That same decade saw many areas set aside for parks. Being largely surrounded by forests in its early years, the city saw little need for formal parks, and no funds were set aside for a park system until the 1870s. More recreational activities were constantly being added, both for the wealthy and the middle class, through the following decades—such as dance halls, movie theaters, skating, and baseball. By 1909, roughly two million people visited Cleveland parks.

As early as the 1920s, the park system was noted as being outdated. In the 1940s, they began to suffer from increased thefts and vandalism. Problems remained as park employees were continually reduced in a response to smaller city budgets. Recreational facility staff went from almost 600 in 1969 to just 134 in 1971. Patrons frequently complained that city recreation facilities were not open at peak times and had too few and improperly trained staff.

By 1977, the city managed to turn several of their parks over to the Ohio Department of Natural Resources, making them state-run. The abandoned Euclid Beach Park amusement park was converted to a state park as well in the 1980s. Cleveland also was successful winning the location of the Rock and Roll Hall of Fame in 1986 from its original location in New York. By the 1990s, the number of city recreation employees had almost returned to the height of the 1960s. The downtown area has enjoyed millions spent on urban renewal, but one does not need to look far to spot the numerous abandonments of decades past.

AVALON THEATER

The Avalon was a single-screen theater built in 1937, opening May 28 the following year. With seating for 1,580 viewers, it would have double-feature shows on the weekends. Between the features, audiences would see several on-stage variety acts such as magicians and performers. Weeknights would play a single feature, with Wednesday nights being known as "Bank Night," when the theater manager would pull a winning ticket on stage resulting in that customer winning a prize.

The theater would close in the 1970s and was sold to the Church Prayer Chapel in 1975. It was later sold to another church in 1981 and underwent remodeling in 1983. The Confirmed Word Faith Center purchased the building in 1987 and would remain the longest, until about 2011. They were an active food pantry and outreach mission, even sending their pastor to Nigeria near the millennium.

THE CLEVELAND AQUARIUM

In the 1930s, Gordon Park in north Cleveland constructed a bath house. It was converted to a trailside museum by the Cleveland Museum of Natural History in 1943 to display exhibits of local plants, animals, and fish. It would close in 1953 when the new interstate highway was built running through the park.

The following year, the Cleveland Aquarium Society, a group of tropical fish aquarists, renovated the building to feature fifty fresh and saltwater exhibits including sharks, octopi, eels, squid, and swordfish. The aquarium was frequently crowded with visitors and received a $300,000 grant to build its distinctive octagonal wing in 1967. Tripling in size, the aquarium went from just 8,000 gallons to 82,000.

Despite bringing new species such as the rare Australian lungfish and red-bellied piranhas, the aquarium began experiencing financial difficulties in the 1970s, even though attendance rates remained high. The City Council approved an admission price increase in 1979 only to find out the building had developed structural problems, forcing its closure in 1985.

Within a year, all exhibits had been transferred to the Cleveland Metroparks Zoo and the building became a K-9 training unit for the Cleveland Police Department. Further structural deterioration finally forced them to leave after the millennium.

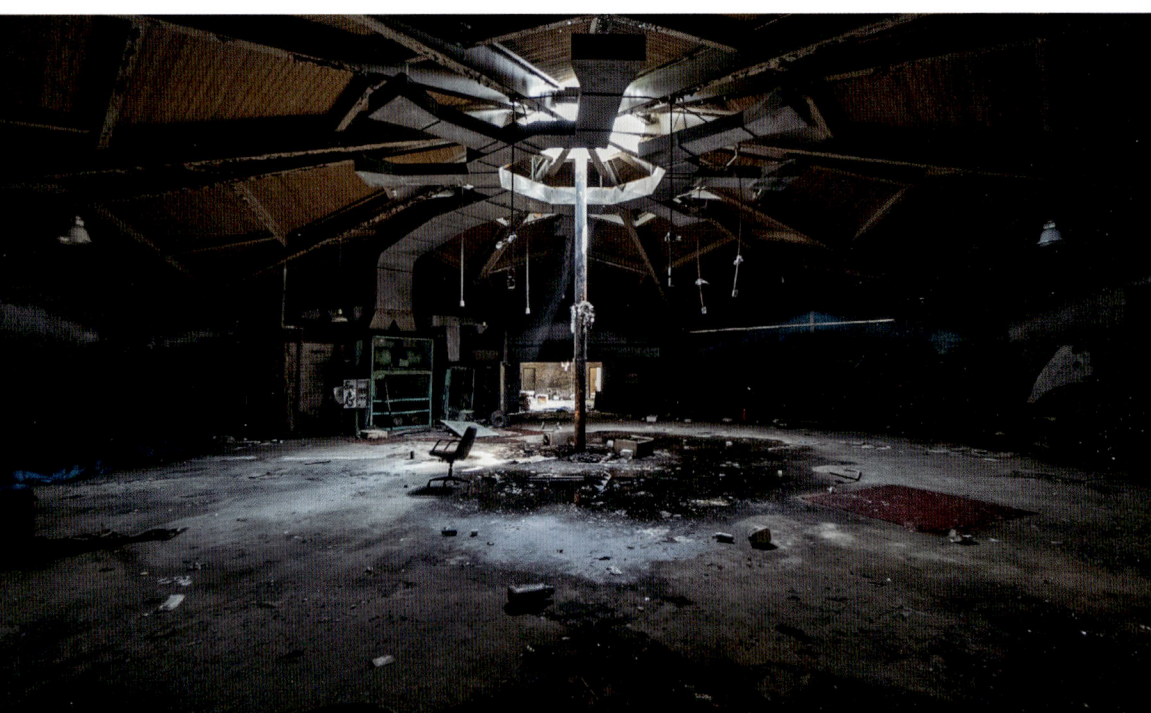

Warner & Swasey Observatory

One of the many products manufactured by the Warner & Swasey Company (covered in chapter 1) were refracting telescopes, which they supplied to many prominent observatories in the United States. After becoming trustees of the Case Institute of Technology, they naturally donated what was to become known as the Warner & Swasey Observatory. Opening in 1920, the observatory was equipped with the company's own 9.5-inch refractor telescope.

In 1941, a second, larger dome was added to the building, which housed a new 24-inch telescope named the Burrell Schmidt. Scientists at the observatory would make many discoveries in the following years, primarily to do with the Milky Way. Finally, though, Case was forced to move outside the city when the growing city's light pollution rendered the current location useless by 1956.

The Cleveland observatory was then opened to the public and a new 36-inch telescope was installed. It would go on to much acclaim as "the nation's finest" public observatory until Warner & Swasey was bought out and closed their factory in 1980, with the observatory closing the same year. It was finally purchased in 2005 by a businessman with the plans to refurbish it into a luxury home, and some renovations began on some of the rooms.

Work would stop soon thereafter when the owner was convicted and sent to prison for two years for a multi-state mortgage scam in 2007. He would again be sentenced to four years in prison in 2013 for his part in a chop-shop ring. The property was transferred to the city in 2011 and has remained abandoned since.

The original 1920 observatory.

–8–
HOUSES

MADISON'S DUMPING GROUNDS

In the summer of 2013, a worker noticed a foul smell coming from an abandoned garage in the back of her business. This would lead to the discovery of the body of a young woman wrapped in trash bags inside. Investigating the surrounding area, police would discover a second body in the overgrowth behind an abandoned home and a third in the basement of another abandoned house, all within 200 yards of each other.

Suspicion immediately fell upon the only occupied home in the center of the bodies, owned by convicted rapist Michael Madison. After a brief manhunt, Madison was found hiding nearby inside his mother's house. A neighborhood-wide search was conducted for further bodies, including at the Elderwood area, but no more were found.

The three victims, whose ages ranged from thirty-eight to just eighteen, had all been lured by Madison back to his home and strangled. The first murder occurred October 2012, while the last less than two weeks before their discovery. Madison was ordered to undergo psychological evaluation and would be deemed competent to go to trial in 2016.

The case would uncover the troubled history of Madison, whose father denied him as his child and left. Madison's mother and her string of boyfriends would beat him and his half-brother. Social workers would report frequent hospital trips for severe beatings, including going temporarily deaf in one ear from one instance. In 1980, he was placed in the care of his grandmother, a heroin addict and former prostitute, before being released back to his mother, where the abuse continued.

By age sixteen, Madison was homeless. School reports noted his hatred toward women, lashing out at any female in authority as well as inappropriately touching a classmate. He became a drug addict and was convicted of attempted rape in his 20s. Despite his unfortunate upbringing, Michael Madison was convicted on three counts of kidnapping and murder, for which he received the death penalty.

At the time of writing, he remains on death row. His house was demolished in 2018. The garage has since been renovated for tenants above the businesses next door. The two other abandoned homes nearby remain standing.

Madison's home resided to the far left. The rightmost home has the basement where a body was found. The grass between is where another woman was dumped.

THIS PREMISE HAS BEEN ORDERED SEALED BY COURT ORDER

Above left: The basement.

STOVER HOUSE

This house in East Cleveland was originally built in 1894. A four-car garage was added in the back in 1959. It was briefly owned by the Administration of Veterans Affairs in 1975 before being sold again, eventually being purchased by Kenneth Stover in 2002.

Stover was raised in Cleveland, later moving to Detroit and becoming a songwriter for Motown Records. He worked on songs for Diana Ross, Bobby Nunn, and Marvin Gaye; his most well-known hit is the original draft of Gaye's "Let's Get It On." By the time he left Detroit in 1981, Stover had provided background vocals for Gaye, as well as releasing an album of his own in 1978. He moved back to Cleveland in 1985 to take care of his ailing sister and continued to work in the music industry, co-writing the Will Smith song "Just Cruisin," which was featured in the film *Men In Black*.

Stover renovated the home in 2008 but would die just two years later. The house was left to his partner, a children's computer software saleswoman, as well as two of his sons. After one of them died in 2015, the house has been left neglected.

WANZER MANSION

Above: This six-bedroom Colonial was built in 1904 by G. Wanzer of Wanzer & Williams General Insurance and Real Estate.

Below left: Wanzer is noted as leading the committee organizing the Junior Aero Club of America in 1920.

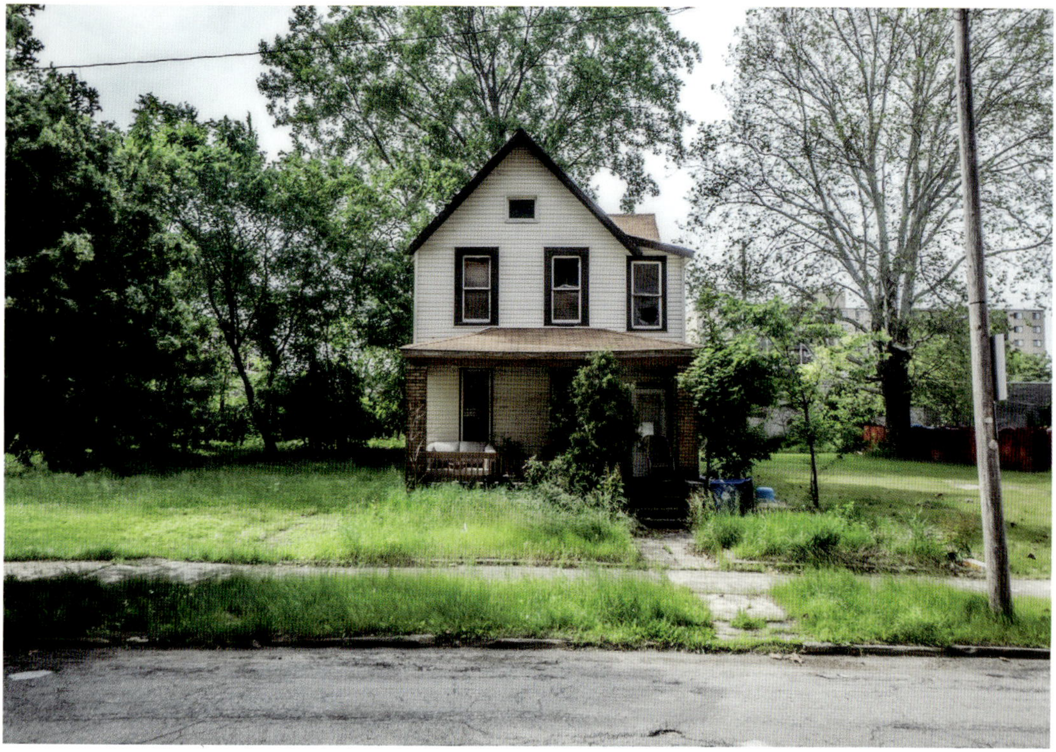

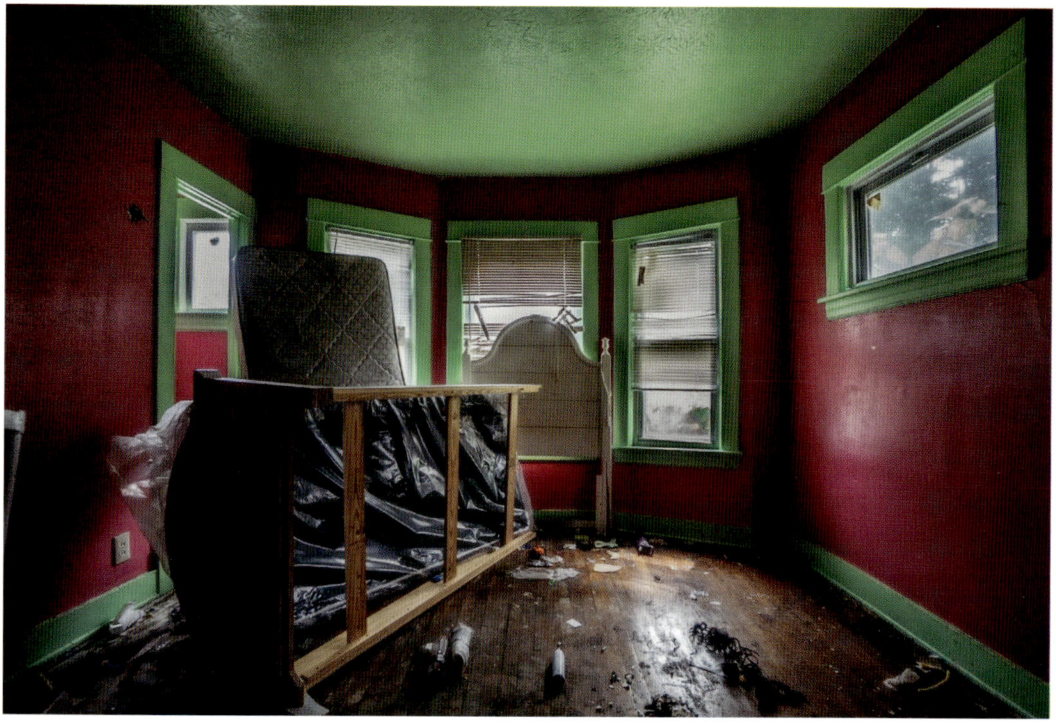

BIBLIOGRAPHY

"Buckeye-Woodland School Profile." *Public School Review*, 26 July 2019, www.publicschoolreview.com/buckeye-woodland-school-profile.

"Classroom Facilities Assessment - Buckeye Woodland Elementary." Cleveland Metropolitan School District, 7 May 2001.

Trexler, Phil, and Tom Meyer. "Hundreds of Books, Valuable Supplies and Furniture Left to Rot at Abandoned Cleveland Schools." *WKYC3*, 2019 5AD, www.wkyc.com/article/news/investigations/the-investigator-hundreds-of-books-valuable-supplies-and-furniture-left-to-rot-at-abandoned-cleveland-schools-gallery/95-7ec1c5a0-7e09-45c4-9998-1e30335b3863.

Chandler-White, June. "Union Investigating Company Buying Castle." *The Daily Record*, 9 Mar. 2007, www.the-daily-record.com/article/20070309/NEWS/303099801.

Jarboe, Michelle. "Levi Scofield's Cleveland Mansion, Long Vacant, Grabs Preservationists' Attention (Photos)." *Cleveland.Com*, 27 Oct. 2016, www.cleveland.com/realestate-news/2016/10/levi_scofields_cleveland_mansi.html.

MacDonald, Evan. "Armed Robbers Stole Dozens of Pairs of Leggings, Other Clothes from Cleveland Thrift Store, Records Say." *Cleveland.Com*, 17 June 2019, www.cleveland.com/crime/2019/06/armed-robbers-stole-dozens-of-pairs-of-leggings-other-clothes-from-cleveland-thrift-store-records-say.html.

"Junior Aero Club to Be Organized." *Aerial Age Weekly,* vol. 14, 12 Sept. 1921, p. 597.

Cleveland City Directory. 46th ed., The Cleveland Directory Company, 1916.

Heisig, Eric. "National Acme Building, Once a Major Manufacturing Site, Destroyed by Crooks and Now a Nuisance to East Side." *Cleveland.Com*, 7 July 2017, www.cleveland.com/court-justice/2017/07/national_acme_building_once_a.html.

Chapin, Frederick H. "ACME-CLEVELAND CORP." *Encyclopedia of Cleveland History*, Case Western Reserve University, 28 Feb. 2019, case.edu/ech/articles/a/acme-cleveland-corp.

Annual Report of the Cleveland Public Library for 1919-1920. Cleveland Public Library Digital Gallery, 1920.

Atassi, Leila. "Serial Killer Joseph Harwell Will Spend Life behind Bars for Deaths of 3 Women." *Cleveland.Com*, 27 Feb. 2012, blog.cleveland.com/metro/2012/02/serial_killer_joseph_harwell_w.html.

Campbell, Thomas. "PUBLIC HOUSING." *Encyclopedia of Cleveland History*, Case Western Reserve University, 29 June 2018, case.edu/ech/articles/p/public-housing.

"CLEVELAND AQUARIUM." *Encyclopedia of Cleveland History*, Case Western Reserve University, 31 May 2019, case.edu/ech/articles/c/cleveland-aquarium.

"Community Circle Apartments I." *Ourparents.Com*, 2017, www.ourparents.com/ohio/cleveland/community_circle_apartments_i.

Dissell, Rachel. "East Cleveland Police Look at Three Cases for Links to Anthony Sowell." *Cleveland.Com*, The Plain Dealer, 7 Nov. 2009, blog.cleveland.com/metro/2009/11/east_cleveland_police_look_at.html.

Dubelko, Jim. "The Battle at St. Ladislas." *Cleveland Historical*, 28 Feb. 2013, clevelandhistorical.org/items/show/596.

Dutton, Frank. "Cleveland: St Ladislas Church." *Frank's Place*, 9 Oct. 2013, frank-dutton.blogspot.com/2013/10/cleveland-st-ladislas-church.html.

Edwards. *United States v. John Henry Reeves, 594 F.2d 536 (6th Cir. 1979)*. 2 Mar. 1979.

Harper, John. "East Cleveland Serial Killer Michael Madison Sentenced to Death." *Cleveland.Com*, 2 June 2016, www.cleveland.com/court-justice/2016/06/east_cleveland_serial_killer_m_1.html.

Harper, John. "Serial Killer Michael Madison's Childhood Abuse Used as Defense to Avoid Death Penalty." *Cleveland.Com*, 12 May 2016, www.cleveland.com/court-justice/2016/05/michael_madison_jury_will_now.html.

Hoover, M.E. "Superior Sub-Branch Annual Report." Cleveland Public Library Digital Gallery, 1925.

Hoover, M.E. *Superior Sub-Branch Annual Report*. Cleveland Public Library Digital Gallery, 1921.

"HOTELS." *Encyclopedia of Cleveland History*, Case Western Reserve University, 11 May 2018, case.edu/ech/articles/h/hotels.

http://swordandscale.com/author/hsutfin. "The East Cleveland Serial Killer." *Sword and Scale*, 5 May 2016, swordandscale.com/the-east-cleveland-serial-killer/.

Keating, Dennis. "Remember Slavic Village? It's Back." *Shelterforce*, 3 May 2018, shelterforce.org/2018/04/16/remember-slavic-village-its-back/. Accessed 16 July 2019.

Netzel, Andy. "Can Anyone Save Slavic Village?" *Cleveland Magazine*, 19 Oct. 2007.

Poh Miller, Carol. "PARKS." *Encyclopedia of Cleveland History*, Case Western Reserve University, 18 June 2018, case.edu/ech/articles/p/parks.

Powell, Janet. *Superior Branch Annual Report*. Cleveland Public Library Digital Gallery, 1976.

Rose, Danielle, and Jim Dubelko. "Sidaway Bridge." *Cleveland Historical*, 2014, clevelandhistorical.org/items/show/762.

Sabol, John. "Nativity BVM Parish Lives on as Part of Cleveland's Slovak Community." *Nase Rodina*, Mar. 2005.

"ST. LADISLAS CHURCH." *Encyclopedia of Cleveland History*, Case Western Reserve University, 12 May 2018, case.edu/ech/articles/s/st-ladislas-church.

Superior Branch Annual Report. Cleveland Public Library Digital Gallery, 1975.

Trickey, Erick. "The Other Serial Killer." *Cleveland Magazine*, 17 June 2012.

Turner, Karl. "Cleveland Man Charged in Shooting Death." *Cleveland.Com*, cleveland.com, 28 Feb. 2007, blog.cleveland.com/metro/2007/02/cleveland_man_charged_in_shoot.html.

Vacha, John E. "RECREATION AND LEISURE." *Encyclopedia of Cleveland History*, Case Western Reserve University, 12 May 2018, case.edu/ech/articles/r/recreation-and-leisure.

Walker, Toby. "Kenny Stover." *Soulwalking.Co.Uk*, 2010, www.soulwalking.co.uk/Kenny%20Stover.html.

Wieland, Ann Marie, and Chris Roy. "South Branch Library." *Cleveland Historical*, 2014, clevelandhistorical.org/items/show/862.

Wilson, Martha. "Smaller Branch Annual Report." Cleveland Public Library Digital Gallery, 1918.

Monday, Carl. "Former Funeral Home Director Sentenced." *Cleveland 19*, 10 July 2015, www.cleveland19.com/story/29513911/carl-monday-investigation-former-funeral-home-director-sentenced/.

Pagonakis, Joe. "CLE Family Records Left Exposed At Funeral Home." *News 5*, 3 Dec. 2015.

"Timeline: Encyclopedia of Cleveland History." *Encyclopedia of Cleveland History | Case Western Reserve University*, 31 May 2019, case.edu/ech/timeline.

Wilson, Lauren. "Residents in Slavic Village Cope Together." *WEWS*, 26 Sept. 2018, www.news5cleveland.com/news/local-news/cleveland-metro/residents-refuse-to-give-up-on-slavic-village-amid-recent-crime-wave.

"Cleveland, Ohio." *Ohio History Central*, 18 July 2012, www.ohiohistorycentral.org/w/Cleveland,_Ohio.

"About Ejila Awori Mission." *KINGDOM MISSIONS OUTREACH INTERNATIONAL INC.*, 2009, sites.google.com/site/kmoejilaaworimissions/about-ejila-awori-mission?tmpl=%2Fsystem%2Fapp%2Ftemplates%2Fprint%2F&showPrintDialog=1.

Hudak, T. "Avalon Theatre." *Cinema Treasures*, 2008, cinematreasures.org/theaters/14081.

"Cuyahoga County Building Projects." *Ohio Architect and Builder*, vol. 30, 1917, p. 6.

"About Us." *First Hungarian Reformed Church*, www.firsthunrefchurch.org/about-us.

"Cleveland City Directory." *The Cleveland Directory Company*, 1909, p. 452.

O'Malley, Michael. "Cleveland Catholic Diocese Announces Church Closures." *The Plain Dealer*, 15 Mar. 2009.

Building Information - Cleveland City SD (43786) - Audubon Middle (1248). Cleveland Board of Education, 2002, Building Information - Cleveland City SD (43786) - Audubon Middle (1248).

Cahal, Sherman. "Cedar Avenue Power House." Abandoned, 5 Nov. 2018, abandonedonline.net/location/cedar-avenue-power-house.

Christie, Les. "Foreclosures Drift to Sun Belt from Rust Belt." CNNMoney, Cable News Network, 16 Nov. 2007, money.cnn.com/2007/06/18/real_estate/foreclosures_hardest_hit_zips/index.htm?section=money_realestate.

Deike, John. "CMSD Unveils Major School Closure and Cost-Cutting Plan Aimed at Modernizing and Improving District." Https://Www.cleveland19.Com, 15 May 2019, www.cleveland19.com/2019/05/15/cmsd-unveils-major-school-closure-cost-cutting-plan-aimed-modernizing-improving-district.

Dubelko, Jim. "Warner and Swasey Building." Cleveland Historical, clevelandhistorical.org/items/show/623.

Ford, Frank. "Myths and Misconceptions About Demolition in Cleveland." Shelterforce, 28 Nov. 2017, shelterforce.org/2017/11/28/myths-and-misconceptions-about-demolition-in-cleveland/.

Green, Joey. Vacation on Location, Midwest: Explore the Sites Where Your Favorite Movies Were Filmed. *Chicago Review Press*, 2017.

Kilpatrick, Mary. "The House Next Door." Cleveland.com, 3 Aug. 2015, www.cleveland.com/cleveland-heights/2015/08/the_house_next_door.html.

Kolson, Kenneth, and Mary B Stavish. "GOVERNMENT." *Encyclopedia of Cleveland History | Case Western Reserve University*, 14 June 2018, case.edu/ech/articles/g/government.

McTighe, Michael J, and Jimmy E Meyer. "RELIGION." *Encyclopedia of Cleveland History | Case Western Reserve University,* 12 May 2018, case.edu/ech/articles/r/religion.

Miggins, Edward M. "CLEVELAND PUBLIC SCHOOLS." *Encyclopedia of Cleveland History | Case Western Reserve University*, 24 May 2018, case.edu/ech/articles/c/cleveland-public-schools.

Pagonakis, Joe. "Northeast Ohio's Most Abandoned Neighborhoods by Zip Code." *News 5 Cleveland*, 1 May 2019, www.news5cleveland.com/news/local-news/cleveland-metro/northeast-ohios-most-abandoned-neighborhoods-by-zip-code.

"WARNER & SWASEY CO." *Encyclopedia of Cleveland History | Case Western Reserve University*, 21 Mar. 2019, case.edu/ech/articles/w/warner-swasey-co.

Wertheim, Sally. "EDUCATION." *Encyclopedia of Cleveland History | Case Western Reserve University*, 11 May 2018, case.edu/ech/articles/e/education.

Wilson, Lauren. "Demolished Homes Bringing Unwanted Guests to Residents Living Nearby Them." *WEWS*, 16 Mar. 2018, www.news5cleveland.com/news/e-team/demolished-abandoned-homes-bringing-unwanted-guests-to-residents-living-nearby-them.

Stapleton, Darwin H. "INDUSTRY." *Encyclopedia of Cleveland History | Case Western Reserve University*, 11 May 2018, case.edu/ech/articles/i/industry.

Simakis, Michelle. "School's out Forever: the Challenge and Opportunity of Surplus Schools." *FreshWater*, 22 Jan. 2015, www.freshwatercleveland.com/features/vacantschoolreuse012215.aspx.

Ott, Thomas. "Cleveland Schools Students Say Farewell as 16 Buildings Reach End of Line." *The Plain Dealer*, 9 June 2010.

Newfield, Jack. *The Life and Crimes of Don King: the Shame of Boxing in America.* Harbor Electronic Pub., 2003.

Shipton, Alyn. *Groovin' High: the Life of Dizzy Gillespie.* Oxford University Press, 2001.

Ferrell, Nikki. "Shaker Heights Man Charged in Three-State Theft Ring." *Shaker Heights, OH Patch*, Patch, 7 Sept. 2012, patch.com/ohio/shakerheights/shaker-heights-man-charged-in-three-state-theft-ring.

J. Mark Souther, "Warner and Swasey Observatory," *Cleveland Historical*, accessed June 21, 2019, https://clevelandhistorical.org/items/show/551.